THE GURKHAS
A Study of Manners, Customs and Country

Dr. R.K. Purthi

SUMIT ENTERPRISES
New Delhi-110 002 (India)

First Published 2011

ISBN 978-81-8420-416-2

Published by:

SUMIT ENTERPRISES
4649B/21, Ansari Road, Darya Ganj
New Delhi-110 002
Phone: 011-23279353, 9810217567
E-mail: sumit_enterprises2007@yahoo.co.in

PRINTED IN INDIA

Published by Sri Lokesh Kumar for Sumit Enterprises, New Delhi-110 002, Typeset by Abhijeet Typesetters, Printed at Sachin Printers.

PREFACE

A book on the Gurkhas their manners, customs and country was done by Northey and Morris in 1928. Subsequently in 1944 major Gibbs wrote on the Gurkhas soldier giving the account of religious customs, social habits and festivals. Later on some more books were written.

Aim of this book is not only to provide to our readers relevant sections of the above works but also literature on latest knowledge on manners, customs and the country of the Gurkhas. Therefore, the selection was also made from some of the good material from internet and media services.

We take this opportunity to pay our indebledness and acknowledgements to the authorities on the subject, and all those friends, librarians and their staffmembers for their kind help and contributions.

Last but not the least my publishers and staffmembers who worked hard to publish this valuable material in its present form, for further intellectual works, and in-depth studies, deserve my readers patronage. Needless to say, our readers satisfaction with the book will be our best reward.

AUTHOR

CONTENTS

1

THE COUNTRY

Nepal is the home of the Gurkha soldier but the term Nepal has a very restricted meaning to the Gurkha. To him it means the Valley of Nepal in which are situated the capital of the country, Kathmandu, and the old cities of Patan and Bhatgaon, an area very roughly 15 miles long by 13 miles wide.

A Gurkha living outside the Valley will always lay that he comes "from the hills" not "from Nepal"

In this short book no attempt will be made to describe the country in any detail. Any Atlas will show the reader that it is a country which rises in series of huge steps from the foothills just beyond the Indian boundary to the main axis of the Himalaya which separates Nepal from Tibet. From these gigantic mountains flow the rivers which add further to the difficulties of travel in the country. With the sole exception of the short rail and road link leading to the Southern rampants which guard the Valley communications in Nepal are restricted to rudimentary hill tracks often interrupted by rivers and streams in spate. This fact must always be borne in mind

* Major H.R.K. Gibbs, Calcutta, 1947.

when the question of furlough and leave or communication with the men's homes is considered.

The Terai, a belt of heavy tropical jungle running along the Indo-Nepali frontier is not an area from which Gurkha recruits are obtained. Many of the inhabitants are Indians of the same type as those on the Indian side. The Tharus are mongloid and are famous as elephant mahauts and as hunters. They also appear immune from the dreaded Ahwal fever which renders the Terai uninhabitable for others except during the cold weather months.

Nepal is governed in a curious and unique way. His Majesty the King of Nepal takes no part in the actual Government but is described as the fount of honour and epitomises the independence of the country. The succession goes from father to the eldest son or failing sons to the eldest daughter to the King. The King is called Panch (5) Sri Sirkar. All power is effectively in the hands of the Maharaja and the Rana family. The Maharaja or Tin Sirkar, as he is spoken of by the Nepali people, enjoys the full title of His Highness the Maharaja, Prime Minister and Supreme Commander-in-Chief of Nepal. The present Maharaja holds the rank of General in the British Army and is G.C.B. The position of the Maharaja is unique. His power is absolute and every aspect of Government is concentrated in him. He is assisted by the other members of the Rana family which has been the ruling dynasty since the days when Jangbahadur seized the power in 1846. The succession to the office of Prime Minister which is hereditary includes the brothers of the ruling Prime Minister according to age and then his sons and brothers' sons according to age. The eldest son does not necessarily, in fact merely would, succeed his father. All the important members of the Rana family live in Kathmandu and it is unusual for any of them to go into the hill districts. Some however are Governors of provinces.

Nepal maintains a minister at the Court of St. James

in London and Great Britain is represented in Nepal by His Britannic Majesty's Envoy Extraordinary and Minister Plenipotentiary at the Court of Nepal. He is referred to as the British Minister for short. The Chancery and Legation are in Kathmandu. In principle it is aimed at that the appointment of First Secretary at the Legation should either be a commanding officer of a Gurkha unit who has completed his command or some such senior British Officer of the Gurkha Brigade who has finished his regimental service. At present the First Secretary at the Legation is a re-employed Lt.-Colonel who formerly commanded a Gurkha Battalion. The Minister is selected from the Foreign and Political Department of the Government of India. In accordance with diplomatic usage and custom all communications between the Governments of Great Britain and Nepal are conducted through their respective ministers. Nepal also has a Consul General in New Delhi. It is often asked why the entry into Nepal by Europeans is so restricted. Various reasons are put forward. One is that Nepal is a most orthodox Hindu Kingdom and that restrictions are necessary to avoid desecration of holy places. The real reason is probably that the Nepalese Government are naturally determined to preserve the complete independence of the country and wish to be allowed to develop their institutions and administration in their own way on Nepalese lines free from any outside interference. They also do not intend to allow foreigners to exploit the resources of the country nor do they desire that uncontrolled and unchecked outside influences should be allowed to percolate into the districts. A further and probably very cogent reason is that inability personally to see how the wheels go round inside the administration of the country will cover a multitude of sins and stifle any adverse criticism of ways and means at the source. It should be pointed out that this restriction does not apply only to Europeans. A passport is required by anyone wishing to enter Nepal be he Indian or European. A further point is to be noted, that hotels do not exist in Nepal and the few visitors to Kathmandu even are the guests of the British Minister, the Legation Staff, or of the Nepalese Government Officials. Special arrangements are made for pilgrims to the sacred places at various times. Friendly diplomatic relations between the British and Nepalese Governments were established by the Treaty off Segowlie in 1815. This treaty of friendship was reaffirmed in 1923 and various measures relating to trade and customs duty etc., were enacted. Under special arrangements and subject to certain conditions the Nepalese Government permits the recruitment of the martial clans of Nepal for the Gurkha (Rifle) Brigade and for certain other formations such as the Assam Rifles (old Assam Military Police), the Kashmir Rifles and the Burma Army. Recruiting is carried out solely under the orders of the Recruiting Officer for Gurkhas by means of properly authorized recruiters.

The Recruiting Officer or his Deputy visits Nepal from time to time to discuss recruiting matters with the British Ministers and His Highness the Maharaja.

2

GENERAL CUSTOMS OF THE NEPALESE

In appearance the Gurkha is decidedly Mongolian, and possesses the high cheek-bones and narrow almond-shaped eyes common to that race. Small in stature—the average height is about 5 feet 2 inches—and fair of complexion, they may be said to bear a strong facial resemblance to the Japanese or Chinese.

Generally speaking the Gurkha is sturdy and thick-set, and he is the possessor of splendidly formed nether limbs, admirably adapted for the rough and pathless mountain country which is his home.

Owing to the fact that there are few roads in the country and, outside the valley of Nepal and the main Raksal-Kathmandu high road, no facilities for transport, the boys and girls of the country are accustomed from their earliest youth to walk great distances carrying loads on their backs, with the result that, as they mature, they are often able to lift the most incredible weights. Their stamina and physique, however, naturally vary according

* W.B. Northey & C.J. Marris, The Gurkhas, their Manners, customs and Country, 1928.

to whether the particular district in which they live is healthy or not. As has already been pointed out, the country comprises every type of climate, from the tropical heat of the Terai to the snow and ice of the higher mountains, and it naturally follows that the standard of physical fitness must vary accordingly. Thus it is often noticeable that the physique of tribes such as the Limbus, who live in the higher temperate climate of the Eastern Himalaya, is superior to that of some of the people who inhabit the lower valleys of the centre. Food supply is another thing which has great effect on the physique of the people, and it is very noticeable that men from certain notably fertile districts are far stronger and more muscular than those from parts where the crops are known to be poor.

Although the simple fare and life in the open air often ensure a stamina and state of health that are denied to many who live in the plains, yet the physique of Gurkhas as a whole cannot be said to attain to a standard any higher than—if as high as—that of some or the hardy races of the north-west frontier of India. Susceptible to chills, and the ordinary minor ailments, they are particularly prone to tuberculosis, due possibly to the fact that many of them have a habit, not only of sleeping in a room devoid of all ventilation, but of covering their heads, during sleep. Although under the regime of the present Prime Minister great progress has been made in the spread of hygiene and medical knowledge in Nepal, yet in the country districts qualified medical officers are few and far between, and the sick have perforce to be entrusted to the care of the local Baidyas, a race of itinerant quacks.

The occupation of the bulk of the people of Nepal is either agricultural or pastoral. Of industry, there is little to be said, for beyond homespun cloths, paper made from the bark of trees, brass, copper, iron and wooden utensils for personal use, but little else is manufactured.

Arts and crafts, such as they are, are almost entirely

in the hands of the Newars, who, on account of their superior intelligence, fill most of the civil posts under Government.

The dress of the poorer classes throughout Nepal consists in the case of a man of the following : a langoti, or strip of cloth round the loins; a thin piece of cloth wound round and round the waist, into which the khukri is tucked, and which, coming down to just above the knees, may be compared to a kind of thin kilt; a thin cotton waistcoat, either of European pattern, or made to fold across the chest and tied outside and inside by tapes and known as a cholo; a small, usually black, round cap, high on one side and low on the other; and finally a pair of stout country-made shoes sewn with strips of raw hide. In addition to the above, Gurungs, and a few other tribes living in the higher elevations, wear a thick rough sheet known as a khadi. This is worn over the top part of the body, knotted about the centre of the chest in such a way as to leave the arms bare and to form a large bag, in the small of the back, in which pots and pans and other odds and ends can be carried. This, however, is never worn in Eastern Nepal, and constitutes one of the few small points in which the dress varies slightly in different districts. The Limbus, Rais, and races inhabiting the eastern districts in their turn usually dispense with the kilt-like cloth round the waist, and wear, in its place, loose-fitting trousers. This is probably due to the fact that they live in a colder climate and so require more protection for the legs.

The national dress of the upper classes of Nepal, and of the people who live in the larger towns, is somewhat different from the above. It consists of the following : a double-breasted garment, known as a chaubandi, fitting tight over the waist, and fastened inside and outside at the shoulders, and at the waist, by tapes. The chaubandi is often made of a double layer of thin shiny cloth padded with cotton wool and forms a warm and comfortable coat. Loose trousers of the same material as the coat and a long length of thin white cloth wound round the waist complete the outfit. The cap is as already described, and shoes of European pattern are preferred to the ordinary Nepali shoe.

Nearly every one in Nepal, no matter what his station, wears a khukri. The khukri is the national weapon of the Gurkhas, and is a short, heavy knife with a broad and very curved blade. It is worn, sheathed in a leather scabbard, tucked into the cloth round the waist. The uses to which a khukri is put are many and various. By frequent practice from their early youth upwards the Gurkhas become remarkably proficient in its use, and competitions are frequently held in which the competitors display their skill in slicing branches of trees and in other feats which demand a strong arm and clear eye.

The dress of the women consists of a bodice (cholo), a skirt (phariya or guniu) formed of many lengths of cloth wound round the waist, and a shawl or veil worn over the head, but leaving the face uncovered. This last is known as the majetro, and is usually of a very bright colour, and the presence of a number of Gurkha women at some public festival or entertainment rarely fails to add a picturesque touch to the scene.

Like their sisters in other parts of the world, the Gurkha women delight in jewellery. Besides being mere articles of adornment, however, jewellery serves a much more practical purpose, for into it are put all the savings of the family, and it may even be said to represent the family savings bank. The jewellery consists, in the main, of large gold earrings (sun), bracelets (balo), anklets (chura and kalli), nose ring (bulaki), and necklaces of various types and designs, prominent amongst them being that known as the tilhari, a heavy ornament composed of alternate reels of gilt and coloured thread.

Up to the age of fifteen or so the young men also wear silver bracelets and plain gold earrings. Every one in Nepal has his or her ears pierced soon after birth, and although the men discontinue the wearing of their earrings as they grow up they take particular care that the holes in their ears shall remain open, and usually place cloves, or small splinters of wood, in them for this purpose.

Rice forms the staple food of the Gurkhas when they can get it, but in view of the fact that it is not procurable everywhere in the hill country, the crop being confined to the larger and more fertile valleys of the lower elevations, dwellers in the higher parts of the country have to content themselves with Indian corn, buckwheat, or millet, from which they make a rough kind of bread, and also a type of porridge, known as dhenro.

The rice, when cooked, is rarely eaten alone, but is usually supplemented with meat, spices, vegetables and, most common of all, the split pulse known as dal. The addition of the last is the means of introducing the vexed question of caste prejudices into their food, from which, on the whole, it is singularly free, for, with this one exception, all Gurkhas will eat everything in common. This prejudice in the case of dal and rice is only applicable to men after they have married, but even this dish may be taken in common if it has been prepared by a Brahman of the Opaddhia class.

Gurkhas will eat every kind of meat with the exception of cows and female goats. They are especially partial to every form of game, such as pheasant, pigeon, pea-fowl and wild pig, while chickens are eaten by all castes save the Brahman and Chetri. Whilst dealing with the question of food it should be pointed out that there are, of course, cases in which certain articles of food are eschewed by certain sects and tribes. To mention a few examples : the Gurungs of Central Nepal make no secret of the fact that they eat buffalo's meat in their own homes, but, on the other hand, they must not even touch domestic pig; while the Ghales will not touch chickens, eggs, or hares. Again, in Eastern Nepal, the Bantuwa, Kulung and Nechali clans of the Rai tribe do not eat goat's flesh; while certain other tribes draw the line even at fish, otherwise generally regarded by the Nepalese as the greatest delicacy of all. Where women are present the food is cooked by them, and, when ready, set before the men-folk of the house. The women do not eat with the men, however, and their share consists of what is left over after the men have finished. As is the prevailing custom all over the East, both men and women invariably squat on their heels to eat. Cutlery is quite unknown, the fingers of the right hand taking the place of knife and fork.

In the matter of what they drink, Gurkhas, again, save Brahmans and Chetris, have no scruples whatsoever, and they have no hesitation in sampling any kind of ordinary European stimulant, such as wine, beer, or any sort of spirits. In their own homes they brew a kind of beer, made from fermented rice, millet, or Indian corn, known as *ianr,* of which they are very fond, but while they also drink a kind of spirit known as raksi, the ordinary commissariat rum, such as is procurable in the canteen of Gurkha regiments, is perhaps their favourite beverage.

The houses of the poorer classes are made of stone and mud bricks, and, outside the valley of Nepal, the roofs are usually made of thatch. Usually single-storied, they contain but few rooms, one for sleeping and one more for cooking being generally considered sufficient. In the front of the house there is usually a large veranda. This is used as a sitting-room, and forms an indispensable adjunct to a home where inside accommodation is so limited. Humble as is their exterior, the conditions that prevail within are of an equally simple nature, for of furniture there is little or none, and it is usual for the inmates to sleep on the floor. Though from a European point of view they appear to be lacking in what may be regarded as almost the essentials of comfort, houses in Nepal are clean and well kept. Surrounded as they often are by gay patches of brightly coloured flowers, they present a pleasing, homely appearance, and one that is in keeping with the cheerful and simple character of the people who live in them.

Although the cottages of the humbler folk take this simple form, the occasional residences of local officials, and such buildings as Government storehouses, to be met with in the hills, are built on much more imposing lines, and with their high whitewashed walls and—too often, alas—shining tin roofs form conspicuous landmarks in the quiet, unassuming landscape.

The Gurkha differs from the people of India as much in appearance as he does in character. His Mongolian origin is responsible for a vein of humour and bonhomie that is not found in the more solemn and austere races of Aryan descent, and his frank and open character permits an intimacy in his intercourse with Europeans rarely to be found in the East. Shy and somewhat reserved at first, he attaches himself very closely to those under whom he takes service, and the devotion and loyalty of the Gurkhas who enlist in our service to their British officers often tend to become what might almost be termed a fault. Coming from a strange country, which, though bordering on India, is so far removed from it in matters of language, customs, and even thought, the young Gurkha, naturally, feels himself to be a stranger in a strange land when first he sets foot in India. His ignorance of the language, which though naturally lessening in course of time, serves to accentuate his awkwardness and seeming inability to understand what is required of him, occasionally gives people who are unfamiliar with him and his ways the impression that he is inclined to be somewhat surly and aloof. Many years' service, even, often seem to fail to create any desire in the Gurkha to interest himself in people, European or otherwise, with whom he is not directly concerned, or who are unable to speak or understand his language. Once his confidence is gained, however, he reveals, little by little, his true character arid proves himself a staunch and faithful friend.

Gurkhas are passionately fond of flowers, with which they delight to adorn their caps and persons. They take a great pride in their appearance, and the gay stockings and mufflers affected by our soldiers when in mufti bear a testimony to their love of bright colours. These last are usually knitted by the women, who enter whole-heartedly into the domestic side of married life, and who take a great interest in administering to the needs and whims of their menfolk. Unhampered by any trammels of caste, the Gurkha women of the hill districts enjoy a greater measure of freedom than is allowed to their sisters in the Indian plains, and they are, accordingly, able to take an interest in life and what is going on around them in a manner more approximating to that of the women of Europe. They are, as a rule, bright and intelligent, and have the same gift of humour and repartee as the men, while those who obtain employment in such occupation as picking tea in the Darjeeling and other tea districts almost invariably prove to be capable and industrious workers. Like their men-folk, they are great smokers, and also share their predilection for rice beer raksi, or any other intoxicating liquor that may come their way.

Life in a hill village is, of necessity, lacking in the amusements open to dwellers in cities, and it falls to the lot of the people themselves to make it cheerful or depressing as the case may be. Fortunately, the Gurkha is in this respect fully up to the occasion, and his cheery, buoyant nature comes quickly to the fore in the production of pastimes and amusements of his own with which to compensate for the lack of other more worldly distractions. A born soldier, the game he perhaps delights in the most during his childhood is that of playing at soldiers, and little groups of children can often be seen drilling each other, or taking part in the mimic battles dear to the youth of most European countries.

It is in the matter of sport, however, that the Gurkha chiefly excels. Living, as he does, in a country where game is abundant and the game laws lax, he has ample opportunity of indulging his favourite hobby, and this love of sport, fostered in his boyhood days, seems to increase rather than diminish with advancing years. The methods they adopt when out shooting cannot be said even to approximate to those of English sportsmen, but they are very effective none the less. They usually stalk their prey until it is within a few yards of the muzzle of their weapon and then fire, with the result in some cases that the animal or bird is practically blown to pieces. In all cases, however, the guiding principle is to get full value for the amount of ammunition expended, and in order to bring this about they usually reserve their fire, until they have manoeuvred themselves into such a position as to get three or four birds in one line.

Neither guns nor ammunition are easily procurable in Nepal, and a licence is required in order to keep them. There are, however, muzzle-loading weapons of a somewhat primitive design which are obtainable in the country, and with these and the weapons purchased in India by soldiers before their retirement, there are but few families in the hills where at least one of its members does not possess a weapon of some kind or another.

Besides guns, which even if not altogether unprocurable at any rate involve a certain amount of expense in their purchase and upkeep, there is another weapon which is much used by the country people of Nepal, the pellet bow. Visitors to certain parts of India, where large numbers of Gurkhas are either stationed or domiciled, may often see them, bow in hand, walking slowly along by the side of some road or stream, their faces turned upward with anxious eyes, in the hope that some unsuspecting bird may shortly offer a target on which they may try their skill. Although his implements are often primitive, and his manner of shooting somewhat unorthodox, yet the fact remains that the Gurkha is a plucky and enterprising sportsman, and when the opportunity of securing good targets, large or small, presents itself, no danger is too great for him, no labour too severe.

Dancing and singing play another very important part in the lives of the Nepalese. In camp, in the lines of the regiments, even when working in the fields, their songs are almost always heard, while on the occasion of any important festival, such as the Dasehra or Holi, they appear to sing continuously throughout the night and day while the celebration lasts. A Gurkha sing-song is both pleasant and inspiriting, and the most downcast individual present cannot fail to be infected with a little of the cheerful and lighthearted spirit which prevails. Seated on the ground—if it be night, round a big log fire blazing on the ground—accompanied by one or two of their number, who beat out the time on their long oval drums, they sing innumerable choruses, clapping their hands in time as they sing, while in the centre the principal dancer slowly gyrates, his feet beating time to the throbbing of the drums. Amongst the Magars and Gurungs of Central Nepal, where, even if they are permitted to join in the singing, the women, except on very rare occasions, are not allowed to dance, it is customary for some of the men to be dressed in female attire. Decked out with the jewellery dear to the Gurkha maiden's heart, with their smooth Mongolian faces and graceful, stately movements, they are not easily distinguishable from the other sex, whose role they are adopting. Nepalese songs, by reason of the constant and irritating monotonous to European ears, but some of them are by no means devoid of **melcody**. This is particularly the case in Eastern Nepal, where the harvesting songs of the Limbus and Rais have often a tuneful and fascinating lilt, rarely found in Oriental music.

Pasturage and cultivation form the chief occupations of the people. Trade is almost entirely in the hands of the Newars, who are also mainly responsible for the carvings in wood and brass which adorn the houses and temples in the valley. While there is nothing derogatory to caste in following the professions of cultivator or shepherd, there are certain occupations which can only be practised by men of the menial classes. These are the lowest of all in social status in the country, and in their ranks are found such people as tailors, gold smiths, carpenters, miners, musicians, butchers and scavengers. These form a separate class of the community, and live a life apart from the rest. In all matters pertaining to food and drink they are considered as untouchable, and no man of a caste superior to their own would ever dream of even setting foot inside their houses.

There are but few barbers in Nepal, and the class of washermen or dhobis, well known in the East for their remorseless treatment of clothes, are also unrepresented, for the Gurkha washes his own clothes in the nearest convenient stream.

Life in a Gurkha village is simple but strenuous. After the habit of nearly all Eastern races, the Nepalese rise early, and as a rule, the countryside is astir by cock-crow. The women take their share in the field work, with the result that very often the whole family sets out in the early morning, the baby, carried in a basket slung on its mother's back, accompanying the party.

During the summer season those who possess cattle and sheep send them up into the higher elevations, sometimes only just below the snow line, for grazing. Here the shepherds erect rough shelters of hurdles and leaves, known as *Goths,* as temporary dwelling places, and here it is that they pass their days, until the monsoon is over, when they return to their villages, often many marches away. Wandering on the hillside one may hear, from time to time, the soft notes of some neatherd's flute, as he drives his flocks slowly across the grassy slopes, and the sounds seem to enhance the unbroken solitude of the scene.

Musical instruments—beyond those of the simplest

form, and roughly fashioned out of materials at hand, such as the shepherd's flute and drums used in accompanying the songs and dances—are rarely seen. But such as do exist are played only by the professional musicians of the country, a race known as the Damais, who besides being hereditary musicians are also the tailors of the country. These supply the music on the occasion of the many ceremonies at which music, feasting and dancing play an all-important part. It is from this class that the bulk of the bandsmen and buglers in the Nepalese Army are principally drawn. There is also a class of professional singing women, known as *Gainis,* in Nepal. These are probably few in proportion to their counterparts in India, and are chiefly found in the lower hill districts such as Dang Salyana. They wander from village to village, together with a few musicians, who accompany their songs, and with their display of tawdry jewellery, semi-Indian dress, and bold, painted faces, bear a close resemblance to the nautch girls of the plains.

One of the Gurkha's great failings is his passion—amounting in many cases to almost a vice—for gambling. This is strictly forbidden in Nepal except on such special occasions as the Diwali Festival. Ordinarily well behaved and extremely amenable to discipline, the Gurkha will lose no opportunity of indulging surreptitiously in his favourite pastime, and the stakes for which he will, on occasions, play are as varied as they are high.

All Gurkhas, from the Brahmans to the lowest classes, may contract what is known as a *mit* relationship with any friends of whom they are particularly fond. The meaning of the word *mit* is friend, and to make a *mit* relationship may be compared with making a "blood brotherhood" in other parts of the world. This relationship can be contracted between men of different classes, tribes and castes, and between people who are already related to one another. Once contracted, the new relationship thus formed holds good where marriage and similar ceremonies are concerned.

Civilization has advanced in Nepal no less than in other countries all over the world, and many of the old customs, relics almost of barbarism, have been altered and adapted to meet the new conditions imposed by a more progressive age. Hence, it follows that certain punishments, which in old days involved the summary execution of the guilty person by the injured one, have been superseded by more humane sentences, usually passed in courts of justice. In former times it was the custom for a husband, whose wife had been found unfaithful, to cut down the seducer with a *khukri*. The latter could save his life by passing under the uplifted leg of the outraged husband, but this was considered so ignominious that in nearly every case death was preferred. Nowadays, however, all this is changed, and, although to this day there are occasional cases where the seducer claims the right to pass under the uplifted leg of the husband, this is merely done in cases where he cannot, or is unwilling, to meet the damages mulcted of him. The summary *khukri* execution, however, is not now allowed. In modern times cases of infidelity are dealt with either through the medium of the Law Courts, or by a local village court of arbitration. This latter consists, as a rule, of eight or ten notables of the village, before whom the parties are summoned. In nearly every case the husband is merely awarded his original marriage expenses, a popular award which is considered to be more than ample compensation for the loss of a fickle spouse.

The laws of inheritance do not, on the whole, differ very much from those in force in India, under which the eldest son obtains the largest share of the property, while provision is also made for the widow and the other children. They vary slightly, however, amongst certain tribes. In the case of the Gurungs, for instance, the eldest son is entitled to the best of the livestock, such as the buffaloes and cows, while the land is divided equally amongst the next-of-kin. Again, amongst the

Limbus and Rais of Eastern Nepal, the distribution of the property of a dead man is usually made by a small committee formed of six or seven of the elders of the village. Here, the largest share again is usually given to the eldest son, or should there be no offspring, then to the eldest surviving brother of the deceased. Amongst the last-named tribes a pretence is usually made of apportioning shares to the sisters and daughters of the dead man, but in actual practice they invariably receive nothing at all, whereas amongst the Gurungs, daughters and sisters, provided they are not of marriageable age, are awarded equal shares.

Gurkhas who, in the performance of their military duties, are compelled to cross the sea, must be granted a dispensation known as Pani Patiya on their return. This restores to them all the privileges of caste and rights, which they are presumed to have forfeited in consequence of crossing the sea. Failure to obtain the dispensation renders a man not only liable to heavy punishment, but also places others, who may have unwittingly taken food and water with him, under the same ban as the transgressor himself.

Nepalese, as is common with all Mongolian tribes, are intensely superstitious, and wizards, witches and witchcraft play an important part in the private lives of many, although the subject is one that is as a rule not discussed with the foreigner, and its symptoms are, in consequence, not very apparent. There are, however, innumerable customs that date back to very early animistic worship, and the prevalence of the belief in ghosts or *bhuts*, as they are called, which haunt rivers and streams, and are known by different names such as *masan*, *pichas*, and the *mathkata* (ghost with its head under its arms), is another proof of this.

Although Gurungs themselves are loth to admit it, there is no doubt that on the death of a male Gurung, a ceremony and dance, in which a gilded bull's head plays a prominent part, often takes place. This ceremony is probably of northern origin, and is probably a relic of the pre-lamaistic religion of Tibet brought down by the Gurungs from the north at the time of their immigration to Nepal. Again, in the month of Kartik (October 15 to November 15), the word *sanp* must never be used for snake, but only the word *ghasarne,* "the creeping one."

The customs and institutions described in the foregoing pages are common throughout Nepal, and are applicable to all the various races inhabiting the country. Manners and customs peculiar to separate tribes will be found described in their appropriate chapters.

3

CUSTOMS AND SOCIAL HABITS

While the Gurkha is certainly not given to making an undue fuss over his food requirements it must be remembered that the Laws of Nepal are founded on very orthodox Hindu caste laws and are strictly enforced in Nepal under pain of loss of caste.

In general it may be stated that any Gurkha can partake of food prepared by one higher or equal in caste to himself. The converse spells loss of caste.

The staple diet of our Gurkha soldiers is rice and in the cooking of rice and dhal caste requirements must be obeyed. They eat meat which is Jatkai *i.e.,* for Hindus. They will eat most articles of food but various tribes have idiosyncrasies the chief of which are as follows:—

> Magars will eat all kinds of meat including domestic poultry but they do not eat buffalo flesh. They keep and domesticate wild piglets which they call Ghar Sungar to kill and eat when full grown but they do not eat village pigs which scavenge and are only eaten by low caste people.

---

* Major H.R.K. Gibbs.

> Any wild game particularly wild pig (Banel) is greatly sought after. Gurungs except Ghales eat all the above and also buffalo flesh.

Ghales will not eat buffalo flesh, fowls or goats but they will eat hen's eggs, sheep (Nepalese variety) and any "shikar" i.e., game killed in the chase. They will not eat any pig except wild pig.

Tamangs will eat any food including beef when possible.

Limbus and Rais will eat domesticated pig flesh in addition to goats, sheep and all poultry.

No Gurkha will eat female goats or sheep.

Above all the Gurkha delights in fish and they will go to almost any length to obtain it. Preserved waters of fishing clubs require special watching if there are any Gurkhas within reach. Gurkhas soon acquire a taste for such delicacies as tinned salmon, herrings and sardines.

As for drinks the Gurkhas cheerfully accept any alcoholic drink available good rum being their favourite. In their hills they brew a simple, nourishing beer from grain. It is called Janr. It is comparatively harmless and when well made it is a pleasant drink. The distilled spirit or raksi is a fiery drink which requires a strong head. Illicit brewing and distilling is frequently the cause of trouble with Gurkhas—particularly women—in India.

The universal cigarette habit has long captured the Gurkha and tobacco in some form is a minor luxury for all but a very few. The old fashioned Gurkha will smoke his "banse huka", *i.e.,* bamboo pipe with earthenware top (chilam). Some men smoke a European pipe.

The normal clothing worn in the hills is simple. For men it usually consists of the lanauti or exiguous loin cloth held in place by a string round the waist. Over this is worn the patuka—a cotton cloth wound several times round the hips and almost reaching the knee. This gives a kilt-like effect. The Kukri is normally tucked into the top of this in front of the body.

The upper classes and most of the Eastern Nepal men wear trousers called Suruwal. They are tight from the knee down and very voluminous in the seat.

All Gurkhas wear the Chaubandi—a sort of double-breasted bush shirt which overlaps in front and is tied both inside and outside by tapes. In cold weather a blanket often sewn into a rough cloak is worn by many. The national cap is universal except in the extreme west where a loose puggaree is often favoured. This cap which may be of any colour but more often black, is close fitting and has one side higher than the other. Eastern Nepalis more usually wear a round Kilmarnock Cap. Really good shoes are made throughout the country and the better off folk wear them. Most Gurungs and many others wear the Khadi or Ainti bhanro. This is a large coarse-woven sheet worn over the shoulders with opposite corners knotted in front of the chest. It thus forms a large bag behind in which all sorts of things are carried.

European coats and waistcoats are popular especially with ex-soldiers while cheap shoes especially, rubber-soled canvas shoes have of recent years become common.

Many men, particularly youngsters affect bright bead necklaces. Most popular with young bloods are the studs made from Indian silver quarter rupee pieces worn in the button-holes of shirts or waistcoats and joined by chains. Gold or silver ear-rings and bracelets are usual for children and youths. The most prized ornament of all is a wrist watch.

The women wear the same clothing with some local variations throughout Nepal. It consists of the following:—

> The Cholo or bodice with sleeves down to the wrists and buttoning in front; the Phariya or Guniu, a skirt which is a long piece of cloth, often with a bright pattern, which is wound round the waist

many times: the Majetro is a shawl worn over the head and shoulders and may be of any colour, material or even a bath towel from an Indian bazaar shop. All women wear a white cloth wound round and round the stomach: in this they carry money, odds and ends and sometimes a sickle or kukri when going to the fields. Jewellery is worn as much as possible and often represents the family wealth. The chief items are the large plates worn as ear-rings and known as Kan ko sun, bracelets (balo), anklets (kuri or kalli), nose ring (bulaki), necklaces (mala) one of which known as tilari is composed of reels of gilt and coloured threads. Another item of jewellery is a large plate of gold or gilt worn on top of the forehead. Rings, are always worn. Sophisticated young Nepali girls of to-day readily take to silk stockings and high heeled shoes and an umbrella is always a prized possession.

As many women have learnt to knit in the regimental lines, pullovers are now-a-days quite common while knitted children's clothing and caps are more and more coming into daily use.

Newar women never cover their heads and always tuck flowers into their hair. Chetrinis almost always wear a donkey fringe over their foreheads. Babies are carried on their mothers, backs and tied into position with a cloth. It is very rare to see a child carried in the Indian style sideways on the hip. When on a journey or going to work men and women carry their goods and food in large baskets called Doko. These are carried on the shoulders supported by a brow band called a Namlo. Smaller wicker-work baskets (Pirunga) are used for carrying food, etc.

The traveller in Nepal will be amazed at first to see the enormous loads which are carried in this style. Quite often old people or invalids are carried for many days in this fashion in a basket.

In Nepal there are no vehicles of any sort except in the Valley where cars and lorries are used to a certain extent. Even there, there are only a very few carts pulled by buffaloes. The rule is walk or be carried in dandy, litter or basket. Only officials may ride pontes on the road up to Kathmandu. In other parts it is possible to hire mules or ponies but very few except invalids or officials use them.

As has been stated in an earlier chapter, most of the trade of the country is in the hands of the Newars.

The types enlisted for the Gurkha Brigade are all of agricultural or pastoral people. The Gurungs and most of the others who live in the higher mountain districts are pastoral as opposed to agricultural. At the various seasons, after harvest, for example, big fairs are held and to them come all the men and women from the countryside to buy and exchange. No Europeans have been able to see these fairs and so it is only from accounts by their men that British Officers can learn of them.

Kunraghat Recruiting Depot and Record Office can, however, provide a very good sample during the period from mid December to the end of March when many thousands of men and women come to draw pensions, Family allotments and to seek news of their men folk in the Army. At that time every type of Gurkha from the length and breadth of Nepal may be seen. In fact it must be the most representative gathering possible to imagine and it is probably not duplicated anywhere.

On some days during the last cold weather the Gurkha population of Kunraghat exceeded ten thousand.

4

RELIGIOUS CUSTOMS AND FESTIVALS

The religious customs of Gurkhas are in many respects based on those of the Hindu system but with so independent a race there are naturally customs and ceremonies which are peculiar to Gurkhas. It is with these that this chapter is chiefly concerned. It is outside the scope of this small book for a detailed description to be given and the object will be to give officers who have only a short acquaintance with Gurkhas sufficient information to put them on the right lines and it is hoped to encourage them to find out for themselves in conversation with their men what they do and how and why they do it.

It is difficult to generalise but an attempt must be made in order to keep this chapter within bounds. Perhaps the simplest way to look at this question is to regard it as bound up with the elemental facts of life.

Birth, marriage and death encompass all men and without food for body and mind together with some amusement life would indeed be impossible.

* Major H.R.K. Gibbs.

The Gurkha is extremely fond of children and large families are the rule. When a child is born the father is in the curious position in that while the eleven days rejoicing takes place he is obliged to eat alone for the first ten. After that the Brahman or other tribal priest comes to perform the necessary purification ceremonies and on the eleventh day is carried out the Nwaran ceremony of selecting the child's name. This often leads to a somewhat confusing set of circumstances as the priest usually only selects the initial letter. The result is that a man frequently goes through life with a number of names *e.g.*, the letter B may have been selected and the mother may call the boy Birbahadur while father may speak of Birsing at the same time it is more than likely that he may be known to his friends as Biru or Birkhe.

To add to the confusion of course he will probably collect a nick name. A big headed man will be known perhaps as Tauke or Naple and a boy with a high treble voice may be called Musa. The solution in completing documents is to find out what the boy's parents call him and if the name differs from the one under which he was enrolled it should be added after the word "alias".

Another curious fact will often be noted, that a Magar or Gurung boy may have the first name of Kami or Sarki. This is because parents who have been unlucky in losing children who died young have called in a Kami (blacksmith) or Sarki (bootmaker) to fix a metal or leather bracelet on the wrist of a new born child. This is considered efficacious in warding off evil spirits and the baby boy will then be known as Kami Gurung, Sarki Rana etc.

Sometimes for the same reason a pretence is made of feeding the new born babe with grain and such a boy will then be known as Juthe *i.e.*, as one who was subjected to a trick or lie.

In our regiments in peace time the father of a newly

born child is given II days "line leave." This is the same in the case of the child being a boy or a girl. The first son is the cause of special joy as it is he who will carry out his father's eventual death ceremonies.

The next big event in a child's life is the Bhat Khuwai or first feeding. This is the weaning ceremony when a formal feeding of grain is carried out by friends and relations. On this occasion the soldier father gets no leave but usually is allowed to have his lights on after "lights out".

Marriage is the next important event in a Gurkha's life.

The customs and ceremonies vary slightly among different tribes. The majority employ Brahmans to perform the ceremony but Gurungs and Limbus and Rais and Tamangs more usually call in their own tribal priests.

Although a Gurkha may be betrothed at a very early age married life does not begin as a rule until both boy and girl are at least sixteen years old or more. One does, however, come across very young husbands and wives at times, this is especially so among Chetris As all the world over, mothers do a lot of match making but it is probably correct to say that the young folk as often as not settle these matters themselves to a degree unknown in India. Among the Gurkhas it is the rule rather than the exception for boys and girls to choose their own partners often without the parents' knowledge. The essential rite in the marriage ceremony is known as Sindhur Halnu and consists in the man putting red lead on the girl's forehead and along the parting of her hair.

Run away marriages are common.

The betrothal (magni) often precedes the actual marriage ceremony (Byaha) by many years.

Even in the case of early marriages the girl will almost invariably continue to live with her own parents for some years. If it is found on checking a man's kindred roll that he has a child wife it will also usually be ascertained that he will describe her as Maito or Maitalo, that is, "living at her parents' home".

If a boy and a girl run away and marry they will in due course seek the parents' blessing and will make submission to the girl's father who usually accepts the position and puts his caste mark (Tika) on the young peoples' foreheads after they have carried out "Dhok dinnu" which means making obeisance.

The first and truly married wife is known as Byahate but he may also take a second wife especially if the first is childless or has no son. If this second wife is married with her parents' consent and with proper religious ceremonial she is also Byahate. If, however, the girl's parents did not agree to the marriage and it is of an informal nature, unblessed by a priest she is known as a Lyate. A widow, except among orthodox Brahmans who do not remarry, will re-marry by the Lyate ceremony. In our regiments only one wife is normally allowed to be with the husband in the married lines. A Panchayat of Gurkha Officers usually enquires into the regularity of the marriage before sanction is given for the wife to live in the lines.

Divorce is permitted and both parties may remarry, the woman by the Lyate ceremony only. The matter is normally arranged with the aid of the village council (Panchayat) and the ceremony (Sinko Panra) as is usual for such affairs is carried out by a priest.

In our regiments matrimonial troubles are normally dealt with by a committee of Gurkha Officers. In cases of desertion by wife or husband and where a third party is involved the damages (Jari Khat) and settlement of property are fixed by this committee.

The Gurkha is a good family man and wrecked marriages are the exception not the rule. It is not uncommon however, where parents have betrothed children early in life or even had the Byaha ceremony performed that the arrangement does not stand the strain and the boy or girl on attaining maturity may contract a run away marriage with a partner of their own choice. In general the Gurkha is a kind generous husband and his wife returns his affection and makes a happy well kept home.

In our regimental married lines much has been done by the wives of British Officers to further child welfare work, and the many maternity wards, first aid rooms and knitting and sewing classes provide ample evidence of the popularity and appreciation of these activities. During the present war detachments of the Women's Voluntary Service have done great work in making garments and other goods for the Red Cross.

Of the many Hindu festivals which take their place in the Gurkha's year it is not proposed to give a detailed description, in normal time they are observed as holidays in our regiments as noted here below: —

Maghe Sankrati approximately mid January	1 day
Basanta Panchami approximately end of January	1 day
Shibratri approximately end of February	1 day
Holi (or Hori) approximately early March ...	8 days
Ram Naumi approximately mid April ...	1 day
Saune Sankrati approximately mid July ...	1 day
Janai Purne approximately mid August ...	1 day
Janam Astami approximately late August ...	1 day
Dashera (or Dasain) in end of September or mid October	10 days
Dewali end of October or early November ...	3 days

Of these the Dashera is of outstanding importance and it regulates the whole of a Gurkha's year.

The form of its celebration varies slightly in different parts of the country but the main features are the same. The Gurkha regards it as the warriors festival and worships Durga the goddess of Victory and the weapons of his profession as a soldier.

The main characteristic is the dancing and general merry-making which culminates in the all-night celebrations on the day or rather night, called Kalratri to which are invited the British Officers and their wives as well as local officials.

The entertainment varies according to opportunity and circumstances from the "Penny Gaff" type to more ambitious dramatic performances but predominant and essential are the age-old tribal dances in which the performers are dressed in Nepali costumes as Pursengis (male dancers) and Marunis (female dancers impersonated by men). These dances go on continuously until on the following day called Mar, when numerous pigeons, goats and young buffalo bulls are sacrificed at the Maula or specially selected place of worship which exists near the hill villages and in Regimental Lines.

The sacrifice is performed by chopping off the victim's head with a Kukri or Konra. The Konra is a heavy curved weapon with a broad head roughly at right angles to the cutting edge. It is always considered a point of pride to sever the head cleanly with one stroke. The rest of the day is devoted to family parties attended with much food and good cheer. The festival concludes with the worship performed on the last day known as Tika when all men put caste marks on their foreheads.

Even if all other festivals are missed every Gurkha makes great efforts to celebrate the Dashera.

The festival of Dewali is in honour of Laksmi goddess of wealth. Homes, barracks and lines are illuminated at night with little oil lamps and gambling is permitted. Most Gurkhas are inveterate gamblers and this festival allows them to let off steam.

The Holi festival with its accompanying horseplay and throwing about of red powder (Abir) and coloured water is gradually losing its popularity and is regarded more and more as a festival for low caste people.

One ceremony of paramount importance is the pani Patiya ceremony which must be performed by all Gurkhas on return from overseas. This absolves him from loss of caste since to cross the sea automatically involves this loss. A small sum (now six pies) is paid and the soldier is granted a certificate. Present arrangements are that this ceremony is performed at Regimental Training Centres. A similar ceremony known as Bhor Patiya is also performed to readmit a man to caste if he has unwittingly broken caste rules by eating with a low caste person. Anyone who has broken these caste rules regarding food however innocently is considered Pani Band *i.e.*, out-casted and is unable to eat with others—even his own relations, until he has performed the purification ceremony.

Deliberate infractions of caste rules render the offender liable to severe penalties including heavy fines and imprisonment besides out-casting him.

The supreme authority in all caste matters for all Nepalese is the Raj Guru who lives in Kathmandu.

From time to time individual Gurkhas carry out personal and domestic acts of worship (pujas) and all Gurkha units will maintain a temple in honour of the goddess Kali together with the Dashera house where all paraphernalia connected with the Dashera is kept.

When a Gurkha dies he is buried or cremated at once. Most Gurkhas now-a-days resort to cremation although Gurungs, Tamangs, Limb us and Rais still often prefer burial. Cremation is more in accordance with orthodox Hindu custom. The body is always stripped entirely naked when placed on the pyre.

Gurungs and Tamangs have a funeral custom quite peculiar to themselves. It is known as the Arghun and the officiating priest is always a Lama assisted by Jhankris. This takes the form of a great sacrifice and feast accompanied by dancing. All close relations of the deceased must take part in it no matter how many years may elapse before they can be collected together.

It is an extremely costly affair but nevertheless a Gurung son is never content until it has been carried out.

In general death ceremonies (usually called Kiriya) for a dead Gurkha can be carried out at any convenient time but normally within 12 months. This point should be remembered when men ask for leave to perform the Kiriya.

The following amount of "Line Leave" is given in Regiments on occasions of deaths: —

> On death of Father, Mother, Wife, Adult Son, Daughter or Brother 13 days: for minor children 5 days.

The Sradh ceremony is carried out yearly before Dashera—no special leave is needed.

One other curious custom obtains whereby two men or women who are not related but may be of different tribes, contract a relationship known as "Mit". This can best be translated by blood brother-hood. It constitutes a type of eternal friendship and one Mit wrill always look after the other's interests.

It automatically rules out any possible marriage between the one man and his Mit's relations.

Normally a Mit will never call his Mit by his name unless circumstances enforce him to do so. Mits cannot sleep in the same place together, nor will a man speak to his Mit's wife (Mitini) until the "Chino Satne" or recognition ritual has been performed.

Satya Narain Puja is often performed by individuals at any time that appeals to them. It is a propitiatory or votive offering to God to ward off evil or to obtain a favour.

5

GURKHA CLASSES

What is a Gurkha? The word is familiar enough but its meaning is frequently very loosely interpreted. A clear cut definition is complicated by the two facts that not every man from the Kingdom of Nepal is a true Gurkha and that there are many thousands of Gurkhas who are not Nepalese subjects.

The Darjeeling district of Bengal, the States of Sikkim and Bhutan, the province of Assam and then Burma contain between them several hundred thousands of people who though, descended from Nepalese born ancestors are themselves born and bred in the districts they now inhabit. To these must be added the offspring of Gurkha Soldiers who have settled down in the vicinity of Gurkha Regimental Cantonments and the flotsam and jetsam who Shave drifted into the big cities, the railway colonies and the industrial areas. To the Recruiting Officer however the term Gurkha means something more restricted. He would perhaps describe a true Gurkha as a man of the martial clans of Nepal. In the normal way recruitment for the regular Gurkha units of the Indian Army is confined to those men only who are of those

* Major H.R.K. Gibbs.

martial clans and who are actually brought in from the Nepal hills. During this war as in the War of 1914-1919 this definition is extended to cover those who have migrated to the Darjeeling district and to the States of Sikkim and Bhutan.

It may be of interest here to record that in 1942 when many Gurkha refugees from Burma found their way into India some doubt arose as to the genuine Gurkha character of these poor people. A number of them united to forward a petition or memorandum to the Maharaja of Nepal in which they stated that they considered themselves to be true Gurkhalis and that they had married among themselves only and lived according to the Nepali traditions and customs handed down to them by their parents. The writer saw and dealt with many of these refugees and only twice did he come across a Gurkha who had married a Burman woman. However these are the exceptional cases and for all practical purposes the Recruiting Officer's definition may be taken as the right one.

Nepal contains many other classes which are not Gurkhas. These will be mentioned later on but for the present we may concern ourselves with the main classes of Gurkhas.

These are Thakurs, Chetris, Magars, Gurungs, Tamangs, Limbus, Rais, Sunwars and perhaps the Newars who are the original inhabitants of Central Nepal especially the Valley.

With the exception of the Newars all these classes have one thing in common, an ancient claim to the bearing of arms and military service. All habitually carry the national weapon the Kukri. The position of the Newars is somewhat unusual and will be considered by itself. The remainder differ in appearance in varying degrees. The Rais perhaps have a more typical mongloid face. At the other end of the scale the Chetri shows a greater tendency to approximate the Indian. All now-a-days can speak Nepali the lingua franca of Nepal though thirty or forty years ago it was common to find recruits who knew only their own tribal language. A curious modern development is that the women folk by nature more conservative and stay-at-home, are now in many cases able to speak and understand Nepali. The vast majority of recruits are quite illiterate and the very few who can write use the Deva Nagri script.

The costumes and customs of the various classes will be touched on in the sections dealing with those classes.

It will be noted that the term clans and kindreds are frequently referred to in subsequent chapters These may best be understood by comparison with the Scots Clans and Septs.

THAKURS

The Thakurs are scattered fairly widely throughout the whole country and are often found to occupy important positions in the social organization and Government appointments of Nepal. In appearance they are generally Mongolian and their dress is the same as that of Magars and Gurungs from whom it is difficult for the uninitiated to distinguish them. Their social prestige is very high and they claim to be of royal descent and in fact are generally regarded as standing next to the Brahmin in the social order. The present royal family of Nepal are Thakurs of the Sahi clan.

The clans of the Thakurs are as follows: —

> BAM. BANSI. JYU. JIVA. MAN. NAVA-KOTYA. SAMAL. SEN.* CHAND.* KALYAN. POKHRELI. SIG or SING.* HAMAL.* KHAN.* RAIKA. SURAJ-BANSI. RAKSYA. ISMALT MALL* or MALLA. RUCAL. UCHAI. SAHI.*

Those clans which are most commonly met with in our regiments are marked with an asterisk in the list above. The clans are often further sub-divided into

Kindreds which frequently indicate the district from which a clan originated *e.g.*, a Bhirkotya Khan is a map whose family originally hailed from Bhirkot even though the man himself may now be living in Sallyan.

A Thakur always refers to himself by his clan name *e.g.*, as Dalbir Chand, Bahadur Sig or Indrabir Khan. A Thakur woman however is always known as a Thakurni and not by the clan name.

The offspring of a slave woman of the old days by a Thakur father became known as a Khwas. A Khwas will always claim the Kindred of his father but he will always be a Khwas and can only marry a Khwas woman, their children in turn remain Khwas.

It is of interest that illegitimate children of the Nepalese royal family are also known as Khwas.

In normal times the majority of Thakurs are enlisted in the 9th Gurkha Rifles but all other regiments have enlisted a certain number. They are most desirable recruits in every way. A Thakur need not adopt the sacred thread (Janeo) until he marries and he can consequently eat with other classes and does until that takes place. His caste restrictions are in any case not numerous nor does he incline to allow them to become too prominent. Generally speaking they are far above average in intelligence and many of them have a considerable amount of education as children. A large proportion attain Gurkha Officers rank.

A Thakur man may marry any Thakurni girl of a clan other than his own *e.g.*, a Sen may marry the daughter of a Hamal, of a Khan or any other Thakur except a Sen.

The marriage ceremonies are performed by a Brahmin and are similar to those of any Gurkha marriage.

CHETRIS

The word Chetri (also spelt Chhetri) is derived from the

Sanscrit Ksatriya meaning the warrior class. This at once gives the main characteristic of the Chetri. He is a more orthodox Hindu than most other Gurkhas and considers himself of a superior social status. He has also a greater degree of Hindu-Indian blood and tradition in his make-up. In old books they are frequently referred to as Khas Gurkhas and their language was called Khaskura *i.e.*, the language of the Khas. It is now known that there were people in Nepal known as Khas long before the Brahman made himself felt in the country. The modern Chetri is the result of many generations gradually absorbing various immigrants from India who were driven into the sanctuary of Nepal by Mahomedan invasions. Without going into details it is probably correct to say that the Brahmin and the Rajput driven by persecution from India contributed mainly to founding the Chetri race. They married Magar or Gurung women and converted some indigenous inhabitants. The ultimate mixture formed the Chetri as we know him to-day. The greater number have a distinct appearance being slighter, taller and darker than the other tribes but one occasionally comes across Chetris who are not readily distinguished from Magars. There are in fact many branches of the Ranas and Thapas for example who have obviously split in the distant past, one stream remaining Magars and the other stream becoming Chetris. The normal Chetri has a more pronounced nose than the flatter one of his more Mongolian compatriots; he also usually has a heavy beard and hair on the limbs and body whereas the other Gurkhas rarely boast more than a few wisps of a moustache even when a grown man. The Chetri is scattered fairly widely over the whole country but he is found in greater numbers in the Valley and more central areas such as Gulmi. Of recent years large numbers of Chetris have been recruited from Eastern Nepal. Their dress is similar to that of other Gurkhas but more of them wear the suruwal (trousers which fit closely from the knee down) than the patuka which is a long cloth wound round the hips producing a kilt effect.

As has been indicated the Chetri is an orthodox Hindu and is stricter in religious observance than other Gurkhas. On active service the Chetri will put aside his caste rules but under peace time conditions he observes the laws as to food. Any Gurkha can partake of food and water from a Chetri but the reverse is not the case and especially in the case of rice and dhall. The vast majority of Chetris wear the sacred thread or janeo but those who do not will eat with Magars and Gurungs etc. Where numbers of Chetris serve together it is therefore necessary to allow them to have cooks and water-carriers of their own caste. The females of this class are known as Chetrinis and can readily be recognized by the donkey-fringe of hair over the forehead. In peace time the 9th Gurkha Rifles is the only wholly Chetri and Thakur regiment having been constituted as such in 1894 upto which time it was an Indian regiment. It is thus often thought that the high social position of the Chetri is responsible for the 9th Gurkha Rifles being the senior unit of the Gurkha Brigade, but the seniority is really due to the fact that the regiment as an Indian Regiment of Infantry became a regular unit of the Line in 1823, before the other Gurkha units were transferred from the list of irregular or local corps to the Line. The Chetri does however enjoy great social prestige and in Nepal he is looked up to as a member of the upper class. Large numbers of Chetris serve in the Nepalese Army, the Rifles and Passupati Prasad Regiments being famous units composed of Chetris and Thakurs. Chetris have always been recruited in other units of the Gurkha Brigade in varying numbers and during the Great War of 1914-1919 as in the World War which broke out in 1939 many thousands have joined. Magar and Gurung Regiments. Numerically they are a very great class in the population. The chief clans of Chetris are:—Adhikari, Baniya, Basanet, Bhandari, Bist, Bohra, Bura-thoki or Bura, Gharti, Karki, Khatri.

Chetris normally call themselves by their clan and

name *e.g.*, Lalbir Basnet etc., but the generic name Chetri is also correct.

A Chetri may marry any Chetrini of another clan.

These are subdivided into numerous kindreds detailed lists of which may be found in the official handbook on Gurkhas. Many of these kindred names are similar in the case of Magars. This is explained by the fact noted above that some Chetris and Magars spring from a common stock before the present caste distinctions became clear. In other cases as the Magars adopted the customs and religious observances of their more orthodox compatriots they took upon themselves the kindred names too.

Before closing this chapter on Chetris there is one class we must consider separately. The Matwala Chetris are the offspring of a Chetri father and a Magar or Gurung mother. They adopt the clan name of the Chetri father but are not admitted into the caste of the father and no real Chetri not even the father, wall eat with them. They do not wear the sacred thread. If a Chetri marries a Magar woman of the Rana clan the children of the marriage will be known as Bhat Ranas.

A development of recent years is of interest as showing the evolution of a class. There are many Matwala Chetris in Piuthan and Sallyan, the most westerly districts recruited by the Gurkha Regiments. The majority of these Matwalas now claim to stand on their own feet and insist on calling themselves Matwralas pure and simple and disclaim any connection with Chetris. They do not wear the thread and will eat and drink with Magars. Their clans so far identified are as follows: —

1. Basnet.
2. Bhandari.
3. Bisht.
4. Bohra.
5. Burathoki.
6. Chalaune.
7. Rana.
8. Rawat.
9. Rewle.
10. Woli.

The above classification does NOT apply to Matwala Chetris from areas other than Sallyan.

The Gurkha Recruiting Depot for Western Nepal at Kunraghat has accepted the position and for the sake of clearness all such men from Sallyan are enlisted under the name of Matwala

Although as often happens in the case of mixed bred people some of them are coarse and undesirably as recruits there are many excellent men among them. Some are so like the Magars they live among that it is extremely difficult, if not impossible to tell them apart. In the past a few have enlisted as Magars without being detected as Matwala Chetris

A difficulty which is sometimes experienced in days of intensive recruiting when recruiters do not personally know the lads they bring in, is that of the Brahman who wishes to enlist. Sometimes the recruiter knows the lad is in fact a Brahman but presents him as a Chetri. This would not matter so much if the lad was keen to soldier and was physically fit. The real trouble lies in the fact that the religious authorities in Nepal insist that if a Brahman goes overseas he loses his caste for ever. In the case of all Gurkhas, on return from active service overseas a strict purification ceremony known as Panipatiya must be performed before he is ceremonially clean. This purification will not be granted or performed for a Brahman if he is known to be one and he becomes an outcaste for life. This being so recruitment of Brahmans is not allowed. Some men have got away with it and have posed as Chetris and duly obtained Panipatiya but the vast majority are found out before they have served very long. The writer knew one Jaisi Brahman, that is the son of a Upadhyaya Brahman who had married the widow of a Brahman, who served in the Army for nearly 30 years and was in Mesopotamia in the first Great War. He was a Subadar Major when he died and held the honour of the O.B.I, and was an honorary lieutenant.

One other complication is that presented by the strict Chetri who wears the sacred thread and in his home conforms to all the rules of his caste. He may temporarily remove his thread either on his own initiative or because he was persuaded to do so by an unscrupulous recruiter, and enlist in a Magar or Gurung regiment. Then he may find life not quite so pleasant as he anticipated and so he suddenly produces his thread and makes difficulties over his food and so on.

Of course he may be punished for making a false statement when his enrolment form was being completed but that does not solve the difficulty in all cases.

MAGARS

The Magars furnish the greatest number of men from any of the Gurkha Classes for the Gurkha Brigade. Of the seven regiments composed mainly of Magars and Gurungs the Magars form approximately two thirds. The Magars are said to have been settled originally chiefly in the Tehsil of Palpa and to have spread over the Central and Western areas of Nepal steadily during the past seven hundred years. Palpa was until recent times a kingdom of its own and was bigger in extent than the present tehsil. To-day the Magars are found in most districts from the hills west of the Valley of Nepal right across to Dailekh in the West. There have been Magar settlements for many years in Eastern Nepal but they were not recruited in any numbers. The great expansion of the Gurkha Brigade in the years 1940 to 1943 has led to a big intake of these men and it has been found that many more Magars are in Eastern Nepal than was formerly thought to be the case. They usually pronounce their clan name as Mangar. A further point of interest is that recruiting efforts and reconnaissances have shown that much country in Sallyan and Piuthan has been newly colonised during the past two or three generations by Magars who have moved west from the more thickly populated areas in Central Nepal. The emigration of Gurkhas both to the West and to the East into the Darjeeling district, Sikhim and Bhutan is a striking proof of the great pressure of an increasing population.

Longer contact with refugees from Hindu India in the days of Muslim invasions has left a greater degree of influence with Magars than with the Gurungs. This probably accounts for the fact that some of them do not appear quite so mongloid and for the greater degree of religious orthodoxy in their customs. These remarks apply more to the big clans called the Ranas and the Thapas than to the others. Taken as a whole the Magars are typical Gurkhas and provide us with some of the finest soldiers in the whole Army. The great Magar tribe is divided into seven clans viz.:—Ale; Bura or Burathoki; Gharti; Pun; Rana; Roka and Thapa. Of these the Thapa is the largest and the Roka the smallest clan. All are equal in social status and inter-clan marriages are usual and normal. A Magar may marry the daughter of a man of any kindred except his own e.g., a Resmi Ale may marry the daughter of any other Magar clan or kindred except of the Resmi kindred. There are however some cross-cousin marriages which are somewhat complicated and differ from those permitted to Gurungs; for instance a Magar may marry the daughter of his mother's brother but not the daughter of his father's sister which latter is permissible for a Gurung. On the other hand a Magar girl may marry the son of her father's sister. The modern tendency is to avoid cousin marriages and for a man to marry outside his clan. This is, however, not by any means universal among Magars. Quite a number of cases of Magar-Gurung inter-marriages have come to the notice of the recruiting staff of recent years. This certainly happened in previous times before the present clan system became distinct.

The Ale clan produces very desirable recruits of fine appearance but they are not very numerous.

The Ghartis are of several kinds and need careful recruiting as many are of doubtful breed. In the past a slave who was freed became a Gharti and as many born slaves were illegitimate children of very mixed parentage it will be readily understood that this strain was undesirable from many points of view. It should be noted in passing that prior to the abolition of slavery in Nepal in 1924 there were two types of slaves. The first were Kamaros who were just the private property of their owners as were cattle or pieces of furniture and could be sold as such; they were usually the descendants of slaves although many were the children of a slave girl who had gratified her owner. All Kamaros were regarded as complete outcastes. The second class named Banda were individuals who voluntarily or through force of circumstances bound themselves as slaves to repay a debt. Such people could and did often work out their debt and become freemen again.

The Royal Degree abolishing slavery also abolished the term Kamaro and established a special clan or caste known as Siva Bhakti. They are officially allowed to marry into the Gharti clan and no doubt in the course of time will be completely absorbed into the clan although the taint of slavery and the consequent aversion persists to-day.

The Bhujiyal kindred regard themselves as superior to other Ghartis. They are mainly shepherds and take their name from the river Bhuji Khola which flows through northern Gulmi. Recent investigations and a study of kindred names suggests a close connection between Ghartis, Puns and Buras especially in the tehsils of Sally an and Piuthan. The Puns are perhaps more localized than other Magars and the greater number come from the north, especially from the districts of Baglung and Char Hazar Parbat.

Generally speaking Puns are very Mongolian in looks and a typical Pun from 4000 Parbat wears his hair long and greased with ghi. A very marked characteristic of many Puns and one shared with Buras particularly of the west, is the wide lower jaw. It is often so pronounced as almost to resemble a swollen tumour on the angles of the jaw. Many come from the borders of Tibet and indeed there is little doubt that some of these are as much Tibetan as Nepalese. The tribes known as Thakalis who carry on a great deal of the Salt trade with Tibet are in close contact with the Puns and resemble them so closely that for many years they have supplied the Gurkha Brigade with numerous excellent recruits under the borrowed name of Pun.

The Rokas are not numerous and are sometimes confused with the Chetri Rokas. The Magar Rokas are found in the same country as the Puns, but mainly in Gulmi, and have produced some very fine recruits though only in small numbers.

The more one sees of the Bura or Burathoki the greater does his similarity to the Pun appear. This is strikingly demonstrated by the large numbers recruited from Piuthan and Sallyan during recent years. They tend to be big, heavily built men and are excellent soldiers. The Ranas are plentiful and widely distributed throughout the country. The Chitore or Chitaure kindred is very numerous and undefined legend suggests a connection with the Rajput Hindu refugees from Chitore fleeing from Muslim invasion. It may be that early Magars who became converted to orthodox Hinduism as a result of their contact with these immigrants adopted the name of Chitore. That however is only speculation. At one time they certainly claimed a social superiority and within the last hundred years a Magar of the Thapa kindred who had lost three generations of ancestors in battle became a Rana. This superiority is not claimed nor is it apparent to-day. It should be noted that there is a Chetri Rana clan.

The Thapa is the largest single clan among all Gurkhas

and its members are widely distributed and greatly enlisted. As is only natural the name of so large a clan lends itself as a cloak under which others sometimes enlist. Given the time and a knowledge of the kindreds of the Thapa clan it should in theory be easy to detect the imposter but in practice it is not so easy as that.

Magars have a language of their own known as Magar Kura which is the same among all who speak it. Not all Magars speak it—the Ales, Ranas and Thapas being perhaps its chief users. It is interesting to note that the women who as everywhere are more conservative than men do not now-a-days speak Magar Kura to the same extent as formerly. During the past twenty five years it has been noted that the majority of Magarnis have come to speak Nepali. Many Puns and Buras speak a dialect called Kam Kura which varies greatly from place to place.

All Magar women are described as Magarni and not by a clan name *e.g.*, Tilkunwari the wife of Subir Thapa should be entered in a family pension claim as Tilkunwari Magarni.

Men are called by their clan name; *e.g.*, Subir Thapa, Manbahadur Gharti and so on. It is incorrect to refer to a Magar merely as a Magar nor should he be referred to by kindred name for instance—Manbahadur may be of the Bhujiyal kindred of the Gharti clan. He is known as Manbahadur Gharti.

GURUNGS

The Gurungs for the most part inhabit higher and more northerly country than the Magars although small settlements are found scattered in other parts of the country. A few are found in Eastern Nepal but they are usually Gurungs in little but name as they have lost the chief characteristics of Gurungs. Large numbers of the finest Gurung recruits have been obtained from Gorkha, Lamjung, Kaski, Payung, Satung, Tanhu and Bhirkot. There are also many in No. I West, a district which is closed by the Nepal Government against recruiting for the Gurkha Brigade.

It is not an easy matter to distinguish a Gurung soldier from a Magar although in their own country little differences in clothing sometimes are apparent to the knowing eye. All Gurungs however, wear a thread necklace known as a "nip". It is composed of 9 strands in the case of men and 7 in the case of women and has 9 or 7 knots tied in it as the case may be. Another minor characteristic which has been noted is for some Gurungs, especially those from the area round the Andhi Khola in Garhung and Bhirkot to have sharper, slightly hooked nose as opposed to the broad nose of the majority of Magars and Gurungs.

Whereas the Magars are mainly agricultural the Gurungs are predominantly pastoral. Most of them coming in from the high pasture lands of Lamjung have a heavy woollen blanket sewn up into a sort of cone. This can be worn over the head and completely covers the shoulders and body to the hips and also any load being carried. It is of an "off white" colour with narrow black and brown stripes. Men—especially Puns—from 4000 Parbat have a similar garment but it is generally distinguished by its wider black stripes.

Gurungs have their own language known as Gurung kura but by no means all of them know it. Their women folk for the most part speak Gurung kura only although of recent years more of them appear to have taken to Nepali. Gurung kura is very nasal as spoken and it is extremely difficult to reduce to roman script. The Gurung describes himself as Thammai or Gurum. Many of the kindreds shown in the lists are probably duplicated owing to men of the same kindred sometimes using the Gurung kura word and sometimes the Nepali word.

Gurungs are divided into two main classes. The first being the Charjat consisting of four clans, Ghale, Lama, Lamchane and Ghotane each subdivided into kindreds.

The second class is known as the Sora Jat. Any original division of this class into sixteen clans is now lost in the mists of antiquity and the class as a whole is only divided into kindreds.

The Charjat Gurung considers himself a cut above the Sora jat and the Ghale is regarded as the superior Gurung of all. It is interesting to note however that now-a-days some Gurungs dispute this and go so far as to state that a Ghale is in a class of his own and quite distinct from other Gurungs. This may be a case of sour grapes. A further interesting point is that many Tamangs living alongside Ghales in Gorkha and No. 1 West have in the past enlisted under the name of Ghale and it As extremely hard to tell them apart. This question will be referred to later when Tamangs are dealt with.

THE GURUNG BERGHA (A BARKHA)

English.	Nepali.	Gurung Kura.	Cycles of 12 years.				
Deer	Mirga	Pho lo	1887.	1899.	1911.	1923.	1935.
Rat	Muso	Chu lo	1888.	1900.	1912.	1924.	1936.
Cow	Gai	Lo lo	1889.	1901.	1913.	1925.	1937.
Tiger	Bagh	Tho lo	1890.	1902.	1914.	1926.	1938.
Cat	Biralo	He lo	1891.	1903.	1915.	1927.	1939.
Vulture	Garud	Mupri lo	1892.	1904.	1916.	1928.	1940.
Snake	Sarpa	Sapri lo	1893.	1905.	1917.	1929.	1941.
Horse	Ghora	Ta lo	1894.	1906.	1918.	1930.	1942.
Sheep	Bhero	Lu lo	1895.	1907.	1919.	1931.	1943.
Monkey	Bandar	Pra lo	1896.	1908.	1920.	1932.	1944.
Bird	Chara	Chia lo	1897.	1909.	1921.	1933.	1945.
Dog	Kukur	Khi lo	1898.	1910.	1922.	1934.	1946.

NOTE:—"Lo" is Gurung-kura for Bargha and in Tibet means "year."

The Gurungs are certainly less orthodox Hindus and indeed were Buddhists entirely at one time. Today while they submit to the Brahman's ascendency they employ Lamas (Buddhist priests) for their more important religious ceremonials. This matter is discussed in greater detail in the chapter on Customs but it may be mentioned here that Charjat Gurungs employ Lama priests (not be confused with the clan named Lama in Nepali and Leme in Gurung kura) and the Sorajats employ Pacu Giabrings as priests.

The age of a Gurung can always be ascertained by asking him in which Bargha (cycle of time) he was born. Every Gurung child—except those in Eastern Nepal—is taught the name of his Bargha and so a simple calculation will give the correct age at any time. Gurungs divide time into a series of cycles each of twelve years and named after an animal.

A Charjat Gurung may marry a girl from a clan other than his own *e.g.*, a Ghotani may marry a girl from the Lama, Lamchane or Ghale clan. Nowadays he may also choose his bride from the Sorajat although in past times this was not permitted and marriages either way between Charjats and Sorajats led to the Charjat being reduced to Sorajat. Conservative Gurungs favour a cross-cousin marriage opposite to that of Magars. By this a Gurung will marry the daughter of his father's sister or the daughter of his mother's brother. A Gurung woman is called a Gurungseni.

TAMANGS

Until recently the only Tamangs known to the Gurkha Brigade were those enlisted from Eastern Nepal and Darjeeling for the 7th and 10th Gurkhas. Major C. J. Morris in his official Handbook on Gurkhas writes that "the home of the tribe is said to be the Nepal Valley and its vicinity, but now-a-days they are found in considerable numbers alt over Eastern Nepal, and large Colonies exist in Darjeeling and Sikhim".

The true position as we now know it to-day is that

there are very large numbers of Tamangs in Western Nepal especially in the Tehsil of Gorkha and in No. 1 West. These Tamangs are in every way finer men than those from the East with whom they have, indeed, little in common. They live alongside Gurungs, sometimes in the same villages and sometimes in small villages of their own. Their appearance, dress, customs and language are so-similar to those of Gurungs that for all practical purposes they are indistinguishable. They appear to have a particular affinity with Ghales. They also carry out the peculiar death ceremony called the Arghun as do Gurungs, when to this it is added that Tamangs speak Gurung-kura it will be realized that in the past many have enlisted as Gurungs and have served many years without anyone being the wiser.

The Tamang has this prejudice against him that he is said to eat beef and so his chances of ever becoming a Gurkha Officer were slight. He will, like Gurungs, eat buffalo flesh. The writer has met large numbers of Tamangs together with Gurungs in the Valley of Nepal and in No. 1 West coming in from Gorkha and found it quite impossible to distinguish them from Gurungs.

Tamangs are divided into two main divisions, Bara Tamangs and Atharajat but any significance in the names twelve and eighteen has now disappeared. They are also known as Lamas or Murmis in Eastern Nepal.

An Assistant Recruiting Officer (himself a Gurkha) who has recently made an extensive tour in 1943 in Gorkha, Lamjung and No. 1 West has reported as follows regarding Tamangs:—

> Besides being found in No. 1 West, large numbers of Tamangs are found in the northern part of Gorkha and a few in Lamjung and Upardang-garhi. Above Arughat on both banks of Buri Gandak River is the real land of the Tamangs where they live in big villages.

In Gorkha and Lamjung they sometimes live in small villages of their own and sometimes in villages with other classes.

LIMBUS AND RAIS

The Limbus and Rais of which the latter are the more numerous have much in common and inter-marry. They may therefore be considered together. These Eastern Nepalese are collectively known as the Kiranti tribe. Limbus are known as Yakthumbas and Rais as Khambus or Yakkas. In peace time their enlistment was restricted mainly to the 7th and 10th Gurkhas although many were enlisted in the Assam Rifles and the old Burma Military Police and all Magar and Gurung Regiments took some in varying numbers. The old Assam Light Infantry now the 1/6th, 1/8th and 2/8th Gurkha Rifles also enlisted many in the old days.

The Limbus are practically confined to the extreme East, that is to the hills east of the Arun River, Ham and Dhankuta being the chief area and known as Limbuan. Limbu recruits are brought into the Eastern Nepal Recruiting Depot at Ghoom near Darjeeling.

The Rais inhabit the country west of the Limbu area right up to the Valley of Nepal. Most of their recruits go to Ghoom but those from Ramechhap and No. 3 East go to Laheria Sarai in Bihar when that Depot is open during the winter. One class of Rais call themselves Diwans but: little is known of the origin of this clan.

Both Limbus and Rais are very Mongolian in appearance and are a shade bigger than Magars and Gurungs. They are fair coloured and have even less hair than other Gurkhas. Although they accept the supremacy of the Brahman they retain more of their original Buddhist customs and almost invariably employ their own priests for domestic ceremonies. These priests are called Phedangmas, Homes or Bijuwas.

The clans and kindreds of Limbus and Rais are

extremely complicated and numerous and owing partly to the system of inter-marriage it is very doubtful if any really accurate list could now be made. One name deserves mention, that of Suba. This was originally a title bestowed on certain Limbu chiefs and to-day it is still used only by the descendants of such a man. The title of Suba is used throughout Nepal for Government officials. For example the Nepalese Officer attached to the British Legation in Kathmandu is known as the Mir Suba.

In our army the Limbus and Rais keep up festivals and customs in practically the same way as all other Gurkhas, although they do not show the same keenness for dancing as Magars and Gurungs. One big difference exists in their marriage rules. A Limbu may marry a Rai and vice versa but the girl will still call herself by her own clan name *i.e.,* a Limbu girl—called a Limbuni—marrying a Rai will still be entered in his kindred roll as a Limbuni arid a Rai girl who marries a Limbu man will be entered as a Raini. Although the young people exercise more liberty of choice than other Gurkhas in choosing a partner they will never marry relatives or anyone of their own kindred; hence the cross-cousin marriages of the Magars and Gurungs have no counterpart among Limbus and Rais.

Limbus and Rais all speak Nepali but they also have a large number of dialects which vary greatly from place to place. They are usually intelligent and quick witted. With this quickness of mind goes a tendency for a quick temper although like all Gurkhas they are above all very cheerful and generous. They appear perhaps slightly more reserved—Limbus especially—than Magars and Gurungs but perhaps that is more apparent than real or because they do not have quite so exaggerated a sense of fun as the others.

It should be mentioned here that the Darjeeling district and the states of Sikhim and Bhutan contain between them several hundred thousand Nepalese the vast majority of whom are Limbus and Rais. In British India they are invariably well educated and have, for long provided the Gurkha Brigade with many excellent clerks. Large numbers of their men and women are employed in the Tea Gardens and responded with tremendous effect to the many calls made for road making labour on the Burma frontier of recent times.

A number of Nepali girls from the Darjeeling district have joined the various women's organizations such as the W.A.C.I., W.V.S. nursing services etc. One complete unit of Nepali girls has been formed in the W.A.C. (I) for signal duties.

SUNWARS

This tribe is a very small one practically limited to the districts on the Likhu Khola river in Eastern Nepal. In most respects they are very like the Magars and Gurungs although they have a language of their own besides Nepali. The few recruits obtained from them are from a clan known as the Bara Thare or "Twelve Kindred." They are excels lent soldiers. Their customs are for the most part identical with those of Magars. The main differences are that they, like their neighbouring Limbus and Rais, eat buffalo flesh. They do not permit cross-cousin marriages and utilise the services of Brahmans for all their religious ceremonies. A Sunwar man may marry any girl of the Bara Thare outside his own kindred or close relationship. The senior branch; of this tribe the Das Thare are not recruited nor do they inter-marry with the Bara Thare.

The tribe of Sunwar should not be confused with the menial class of goldsmiths known as Sunars.

NEWARS

The Newars are considered to be the aboriginal inhabitants of the Valley of Nepal and to-day they form the bulk of its population. Their glory as a race has departed and their aristocracy was all but exterminated by the conquering Gurkhas under prithwi Narayan in the middle of the eighteenth century. Newars are now-a-days predominantly merchants, artisans and cultivators. From early times they were both artistic and religious and it is to them that Nepal owes the glorious wood and metal work which is so marked a feature of the Valley. Many Newars early on became orthodox Hindus but originally they were mainly Buddhists. A curious blend of the two religions exists even to-day but Brahmanic Hinduism is slowly and surely displacing the last traces of Buddhism. To-day the Newars are divided into four classes, to make a somewhat arbitrary distinction. The upper class consists of the priestly Brahman division largely concentrated in the cities of the Valley. Men of this class are either engaged entirely in religious occupations in the many temples or clerical and such administrative occupations as are now open to them *e.g.*, the present Private Secretary to the Maharaja is a Newar and is known as the Bada Kaji. Next come the traders and merchants who though predominating in the Valley also carry on their trade throughout the country.

Then come the artisans skilled as carpenters, wood carvers, metal workers, makers of bells and so on. The largest class, the Jyapus, is composed of the cultivators who make the Valley one of the most fertile areas in the whole world. Consciously or unconsciously this division of the Newars has followed the Hindu caste system of class segregation. There has even come to exist a class known as Sresta corresponding to the Hindu military class known as Ksatriya or among Gurkhas as Chetri. It is mainly from this class that considerable numbers of soldiers have come. In normal times fewer Newars were enlisted than was formerly the case but as in the Great War of 1914 to 1919 so again now many have come forward to enlist and make excellent soldiers. Many Newars have the sub-caste name Pradhan.

In appearance the Newars vary greatly and

undoubtedly in many cases we can see the influence of Indian blood. As a whole they are taller and of slighter build than Magars and Gurungs. Many of them are of very fair complexion. The Mongol characteristics are evident both in their appearance and in their own language. Many have enlisted as Magars and have remained undetected. Their dress varies with the locality and in the Valley the tight trousers known as Suruwal with the "chaubandi" coat forms the normal attire. The Nepali cap is universal for men. This is a round brimless cap of any colour, often black, with one side higher than the other. The women, spoken of as Newarnis, dress in gay coloured bodice and skirt with a shawl worn over the shoulders but not over their heads. They are very fond of jewellery especially on their ears and always tuck a flower into the knot of their hair which is drawn back over the head to the nape of the neck.

MISCELLANEOUS TRIBES

In addition to the tribes already dealt with some others are worthy of mention, some because the great expansion of the army of recent years has been responsible for their enrolment and others because they have always been enlisted for specific trades and occupations.

The Sherpas of Eastern Nepal have always been known as excellent porters and it was from among them that the famous "Tigers" were selected for the Everest and other expeditions. The Sherpas come from the districts on the East Nepal—Tibet borders and there are also many in Darjeeling. They are Buddhists of an easy going kind who will eat and drink pretty well anything. Their fondness for drink and gambling sometimes leads them into trouble unless they are under strict supervision but their fine physique is a great point in their favour and some have proved good soldiers. In the past they were not usually enlisted but some enlisted under the name of Lamas.

In the Darjeeling district there are many Lepchas and Bhotiyas who are not Gurkhas but have been enlisted as mess waiters and as artisans of different kinds. They are cheerful people and make excellent private servants but are not enlisted as soldiers.

Dotiyals come from the extreme West of Nepal from the districts of Silgarhi and Doti. They also inhabit the British India districts of Kumaon. These Dotiyals are not soldiers but are enrolled as porters, an occupation for which they are well fitted and which is their normal means of livelihood.

The Tharus are a mixed race of Mongolian descent who have lived in the Terai for many generations. They are not soldiers but elephant mahouts and porters. They appear to be among the few who are immune from the deadly awal fever of the Terai.

Sarkhis (bootmakers) and Kamis or Lohars (blacksmiths) are well known in all Gurkha regiments where they are enlisted for their particular occupations.

Damais are tailors and musicians who are enlisted only in those capacities. None of the above are true Gurkhas and are not fighting men.

There are other menial classes such as the miners (agri), potters (kumhal) and boatmen (manji) who are not usually met with as they are not enlisted as soldiers.

No menial castes may eat with the fighting castes and should they do so the higher caste man is at once considered "Pani band" i.e. out-casted until he and all who may have eaten with him have performed the proper religious ceremonies which will enable them to regain their caste. It is this point which has to be watched so carefully by the Recruiting Staff since it affects all units and all individuals passing through the Depots, as in the case of an infectious disease all "contacts" have to be isolated and endless trouble is caused. Despite all precautions cases do occur particularly when an unscrupulous recruiter is determined to lie.

Finally, a Gurkha soldier will occasionally be met who is known as a Giri. They are not numerous but are enlisted at times. There are three kinds of Giris. The first class are Jogi Giris also called Sanyasi Giris; these do not have the small pigtail and are religious mendicants who have performed the Sanyas Dharam *i.e.,* dedicated themselves to mendicancy. They are not enlisted. The second class are a sort of Chetri. They wear the thread but will eat food prepared by Magars and Gurungs although these will not eat the food of Giris. They are said to be mainly confined to East Nepal. The third class are Matwala Giris who do not wear the sacred thread; they too will eat food prepared by Magars and Gurungs but the converse does not hold. They are to be found in East Nepal and also in Tahsil No. 4 West. Both the second and third classes are enlisted if otherwise found suitable.

6

THE PEOPLE AND THEIR LANGUAGES

To the Western European nothing could be more astonishing than the diversity of language which he would find in Nepal. In a population of under six millions in all there are spoken at least a score, if not indeed a still greater number, of languages, all mutually unintelligible, and some broken up again into numerous and often very different dialects. Even within the limits of a single valley there may be a village the inhabitants of which speak a language completely unintelligible to their neighbours in the next village a mile or two away.

The origin of this diversity is to be found firstly in the various migrations which have brought the present population into the country, and secondly in the difficulties of intercommunication imposed by the geographical features.

All observers have agreed that the bulk of the population display physical features which justify us in classing them as a whole as belonging to Mongolian or Mongoloid stock.

But it is likely that the Mongolians, whose advance

down the southern slopes of the Himalaya appears to have taken place at a comparatively late period, may have overlaid an earlier population. What this was we cannot say with certainty. But recent researches have shown that in all probability the earlier inhabitants of North India belonged to the Austro-Asiatic race, or at least spoke Austro-Asiatic languages. As will be seen later, some authorities also include in this family certain of the many languages of Nepal. It is therefore probable that the speakers of these are the descendants, however much mingled in blood with the subsequent Mongolian invaders, of the original inhabitants whom those invaders found already in the country.

Tribes of Mongoloid stock are found along the whole length of the Himalaya with languages closely akin to those of the Tibetans on the northern side, while farther east similar peoples have driven the older Austro-Asiatic-speaking populations out of most of Burma and Siam.

This immigration of Mongolians is still to some extent proceeding, since there is a certain influx of people from Tibet into the higher valleys of Nepal. But the beginnings of the process probably go back to an early period and may well have preceded the first flow into the country of the third main component of the population.

These are the Aryan speakers from India proper, who, as we shall see, entered Nepal probably both from the west, along the hills, and from the plains on the south. Although certainly much less in number than the Mongolian element, they have yet affected the physical type to an appreciable degree, and among certain classes, such as Chetris, men and women may be seen of a type approximating to that usually found on the Gangetic plain.

It is doubtful what credence should be placed in the tradition that the Newars, a race of Mongoloid appearance, and, as we shall see, with a language akin to that of Tibet, are of Dravidian stock and came originally to the valley from South India. But it must be remembered that the Dravidian languages once extended farther to the north, and that even to-day isolated representatives of this family reach lip through Orissa into Bihar as far north as the Ganges itself.

Amidst this number of tribes of different speech and often of diverse origin there are to-day generally recognized eleven main divisions, arranged here in a descending order of social standing:

Brahmans
Thakurs
Chetris or Khas
Gurungs
Magars
Newars
Limbus
Rais
Sunwars
Murmis
Tharus.

More detailed descriptions of these will be found in subsequent chapters. But it may be noted that the conquest of Nepal by the house of Gurkha, and the subsequent consolidation and extension of a central Government, has resulted in the name of Gurkha being generally applied to all the inhabitants of Nepal.

We can now consider the distribution of the languages spoken by the different sections of the populations; and in so doing make clear the origin of that one which, as the language of administration, has become the *lingua franca* of the whole country, and is destined eventually to exterminate all the others.

It has already been suggested that these multifarious languages belong to at least three distinct families of speech—(a) Munda, a division of Austro-Asiatic; (b) Tibeto-Burman; (c) Indo-Aryan. It may be well to add here a note of warning: identity of language does not necessarily connote identity of race; and, as we have seen, in Nepal itself the aborigines, of whatsoever race, largely changed their language for that of the Mongolian invaders, while we may to-day observe the same process as the language of the latter is gradually replaced by the Aryan.

To the earliest or Munda stratum, J. Przyluski ascribes the following:

Darmiya
Byangsi
Caudangsi
Khambu
Yakha
Vayu
Limbu
Thami

The Austro-Asiatic is a diverse family of languages spoken from Annam in the east to the plateau of Chhota Nagpur in the west. Of this family the Munda group is a sub-division spoken at one time over the whole of Northern India, but now confined to the plateau of Chhota Nagpur and possibly a few isolated dialects, on the southern race of the Himalaya, not only in Nepal itself, as noted above, but also further to the west. These languages are, however, so much mixed with elements from those which have for long been supplanting them, namely, Indo-Aryan and especially Tibeto-Burman, that some scholars have classified them as belonging, not to the Munda, but to the Tibeto-Burman family.

Among the latter, in any case, the following are usually included :

Gurung
Magar
Newari
Sunwar
Murmi.

Of these Newari is the most important; for it alone possesses a literature. Referring to it, Sten Konow says: "Buddhism was introduced into Nepal at a very early date. The sacred books of the Nepalese Buddhists were written in Sanskrit, and that language became the principal vehicle of Nepalese literature. Newari was, however, also used for literary purposes at a comparatively early period. Most Newari books are, according to Hodgson, translations and comments from and upon the Sanskrit literature current in Nepal. We also find works on the history of the country, Sanskrit-Newari dictionaries, and so forth, and in some Nepalese plays stage directions are written in Newari. The oldest Newari manuscript as yet known was written in the fourteenth century. It is a Vamsavali, and chronicles the chief events in the history of Nepal from A.D. 1056 till 1388. We do not know how long before that time Newari had been used as a literary language, and, on the whole, our knowledge about Newari literature is very unsatisfactory."

The Tibeto-Burman family of languages are those spoken by some twenty millions of persons throughout Tibet and a large part of Burma, and related ultimately with Chinese. The speakers of these languages have, since an early period, gradually been overflowing on to the south side of the Himalaya, where they have overlaid the languages of the earlier Munda speakers.

In addition to the languages which have been provisionally classified as Munda or Tibeto-Burman, there are also many others, of which practically nothing is known but the names, e.g. Kamkura, and Raj, with its, at least, ten different dialects.

We come now to the third and most important family, the Indo-Aryan. At some time during the second millennium B.C. there appeared in the passes of the north-west people who called themselves Aryans. The language spoken by them had no connection with either of the two families we have been considering. On the contrary, it belongs to the great Indo-European family which comprises to-day most of the languages of Europe, including our own and, outside Europe, those of Armenia and Persia. Documents written in Indo-European languages have been found even as far east as Chinese Turkestan. The Aryans, when they appeared on the borders of India, had but recently parted company with the Iranians, from whose tongue are descended the Iranian languages spoken to-day from the Caucasus to the Pamirs, and from the Caspian to Baluchistan, including, of course, Persian itself. Both these groups—the Iranians left north of the Hindu Kush, and the Aryans, now beginning the invasion of India—spoke languages which, at that time, very closely resembled each other.

That of the Indo-Aryans is known to us first in the hymns of the Rig-Veda. Preserved as a literary language, it was eventually standardized under the name of Sanskrit. With the spread of Aryan conquest and the carrying of Aryan civilization over India, the language spoken by the conquerors, and by degrees imposed upon and learnt by the populations they conquered, underwent inevitable evolution, and has developed, in the course of centuries, into the modern so-called Indo-Aryan languages of India, which, amongst innumerable dialects, include Kashmiri, Sindhi, Panjabi, Hindi and Urdu, Bengali Assamese, Oriya, Gujarati, and Marathi. Later emigrations from India carried representatives of these languages in the south into Ceylon, as Singhalese, while in the north-west the wanderings of Gypsy bands have brought it back to Europe, Where it still survives in the languages spoken at the present day by the Gypsies.

As the Aryans spread over the plains of India, so also they found their way south-east along the southern slopes of the Himalaya, and to-day an unbroken chain of Indo-Aryan dialects, showing certain characteristics in common and merging by almost imperceptible degrees one into the other, stretches from Chitral in the north-west, through Gilgit and Kashmir, along the whole southern slopes of the Himalaya through the Simla Hills, Garhwal and Kumaon, to Nepal.

These hill dialects, once carried into the valleys where they are now spoken, have, doubtless, been open from time to time to the influence of their relations in the plains, so that the hill dialects north of the Panjab have certain features in common with Panjabi; those north of the Hindi-speaking area have certain features in common with Hindi. Other historical accidents, such as the retreat of considerable numbers of Rajputs into the mountains under Mohammedan pressure, may have led to some further mixture of dialect. And subsequently to the extension of Aryan languages and influences over the Gangetic plain, similar forces must have been exercised by the political and cultural relations of the valley of Nepal itself with the country lying to the south. Indeed, immediately to the south, at the junction of the Ganges and the Son, was the city of Pataliputra—the modern Patna—at one time capital of the empire of Asoka, whose monuments have been found inside the boundaries of modern Nepal and who, according to tradition, visited that country in 249 B.C., and later founded the city of Patan to replace the older capital of Manju Patan. It follows, therefore, that the Indo-Aryan language first known to the inhabitants of the valley was probably that of the capital city of Pataliputra, or of the plains lying between it and the Terai, which later developed into the group of dialects classed as Bihari. One of these, Maithili, immediately to the south of the eastern Nepal Terai, developed a literature dating from the fifteenth century, and traces of its influence can be seen in the dialects of the Terai and in the Valley itself. It was not from here, however, that the Indo-Aryan dialect, now the language of Government and administration throughout the kingdom of Nepal, variously called Khaskura, Parbatiya, Gorkhali, or officially and preferably, Nepali, entered the country. For Nepali has as its closest linguistic relation, not the Indo-Aryan dialects to its south on the plains, but that on the west, namely Kumaoni. It is thus the most easterly of those Indo-Aryan languages which made their way along the foothills of the Himalaya. It must have been brought, eventually, into the valley of Nepal by those movements of conquest and infiltration from west to east which culminated in the conquest of Kathmandu by the house of Gurkha.

Nepali was not committed to writing until, as the language of the rulers, it reached the valley of Nepal; and up to the present no documents in it have come to light which are very much more than one hundred years old, though it may be hoped that others will still be found in the libraries of Kathmandu and elsewhere.

The direct connection of Nepali with the Indo-Aryan languages of the western Himalaya is indicated by early sound-charges common to both but not shared by the languages of the plains. For example, in Sanskrit words containing a *t* following an *n* the *t* has been changed to *d,* while on the plains east of the Panjab it has remained unchanged : *e.g.* Sanskrit *tantuh,* "thread," becomes Lahnda land, Nepali *tado,* "bowstring," while Hindi has tat.

On the other hand, once these dialects had made their way along the mountains their speakers established closer relations with the people of the neighbouring plains, and it came about that the subsequent development progressed along lines similar to those of the adjoining plains. Thus, in Hindi an original short vowel followed by a double consonant was lengthened, and one of the consonants dropped; whereas to the west, in Panjabi, such a group remained unchanged. Since this was a change which occurred at a date comparatively late, when the mountain languages had already made their way far to the east, we need not be surprised to find it in Nepali, whereas those mountain dialects in touch with Panjabi do not show it. For example, Sanskrit *hastah,* "hand," becomes in Panjabi *hatth,* but in Hindi *hath,* and in Nepali *hat.*

Being brought into close contact with languages of Tibeto-Burman origin and imposed upon the speakers of these languages, Nepali has not escaped influence from them. No doubt numerous words, and in particular idioms, in the language owe their origin to this source.

One other point must be noted. Reference was made above to the standardization of the early Indo-Aryan spoken language in a literary form called Sanskrit. The spoken language, as we have seen, continued to change and develop, but the literary language, as far as its outward form was concerned, remained unchanged. In the same way Latin, developing as a spoken language variously into Italian, Spanish, French, and so on, as a literary language continued to be used unaltered into the Middle Ages and even to the present day in the Roman Church. A learned language, such as this, used side by side with a popular tongue, could not fail to influence it, and actually the modern Romance languages contain not only words inherited from their original Latin ancestor, such as French *frele*, "weak," inherited from Latin *fragilis*, but also immense numbers of words borrowed from the literary, as French fragile borrowed, as opposed to inherited, from Latin *fragilis*.

Exactly the same state of affairs is found in India and the Indo-Aryan languages. Their basic vocabulary consists of words inherited from the original spoken Sanskrit, many of them much altered in the course of centuries. At the same time they have been filled with an ever-increasing number of words borrowed from literary Sanskrit. So in Nepali we have common words, like those already quoted, inherited from Sanskrit, while others, and particularly words of religious significance since it was the Brahmans who learnt Sanskrit, have been borrowed. For example, words like *deuta*, "a god," *puja*, "worship," *pavitra*, "pure," have been borrowed and not inherited from the Sanskrit *devata*, *pujay* and pavitra respectively. The constant repetition of poems, often with a religious basis, and containing large numbers of such originally literary words, has led to their eventual adoption in the common speech, although not necessarily and exclusively in a religious sense. In other cases the fear of naming a dangerous animal by its proper name, or the desire to propitiate it by according it its high-sounding Sanskrit title, has led to the substitution of the popular inherited word by its Sanskrit original. Thus the snake is now no longer generally termed *sap* (inherited word), but *sarpa* (borrowed Sanskrit original). And generally with the increase of printed works this incorporation of learned words is proceeding apace.

7

RELIGION AND FESTIVALS

At one time Buddhism was the predominant religion of Nepal, but at the present day the great majority of the people profess the Hindu faith, although, apart from the inhabitants of the valley, they cannot be considered as very strict followers of that religion.

Buddhism, so far as it exists at the present time, has been very much modified by the adoption or retention of many Hindu doctrines and practices which have, naturally, been introduced into the country by outside influence. As is to be expected, the people living in the north and north-eastern parts of the country profess a religion which is but little removed from the Buddhism of present-day Tibet, although they too on occasion pay homage to the various Hindu deities and are classed officially as Hindus.

As an instance of this curious blending of Hinduism and Buddhism, it is interesting to note that situated in the very cloisters of Swayambhunath—the most revered Buddhist shrine in the whole of Nepal, and yearly visited

* W.B. Northey & C.J. Marris, The Gurkhas, their Manners, customs and Country, 1928.

by many pilgrims from Tibet and elsewhese—there is to be found a purely Hindu temple. This temple is dedicated to Devi Sitla, whose assistance is deemed necessary for recovery from smallpox, and was built at a time when that disease—at one time very common in Nepal—was rampant in the valley. The Buddhists of that time, finding that they were no more immune from the disease than their neighbours of the Hindu persuasion, and having no appropriate deity of their own whose powers could be invoked in connection with this specific disease, had no scruples in building a new temple and dedicating it to the Hindu god. The temple is still in existence, and a visit to it is now considered an integral part of the elaborate ceremonial attendant upon a visit to this famous place of pilgrimage.

More examples of a similar nature could easily be cited, but the foregoing is sufficient to show the curious admixture of the two once rival religions which has taken place and is still continuing, but always towards the eventual extinction of Buddhism.

The rulers of Nepal are, of course, strict followers of the Hindu faith in all its details. Their example is primarily responsible for the fact that the majority of the people have adopted Hinduism as the fashionable cult, although, apart from the dwellers in the actual valley of Nepal, they cannot be said to be strict followers, either of this, the Buddhist, or any other religion.

Although somewhat lax in their religious observances, these mountain peoples are very fond of the displays of dancing, music, and general hilarity which are considered an indispensable adjunct to the majority of the Hindu festivals. It thus follows that these festivals, which differ but little from those practised in Hindustan, are celebrated throughout the length and breadth of the country with great enthusiasm.

Of these festivals, by far the most important is that

known as Dasehra, which commemorates the victory of the goddess Durga over the monster Maheshur.

This festival, which lasts for ten days, usually takes place early in October, but the actual date for its commencement is determined by astrologers, and is dependent upon the position of the moon.

From the Gurkha point of view, the first six days, known technically as *Saradh*, are considered of comparatively little importance, but during this period a certain amount of ceremonial, which entails also much singing and dancing and, let it be noted, the usual libations, without which no such ceremony can be considered complete, takes place.

On the first day of the festival the Brahmans sow barley at the spot where they worship and sprinkle it daily with sacred water, but it is the last four days of this festival—known respectively as *Phulpati, Astami, Naumi* and *Dasatmi*—which are considered the most important in the whole Hindu calendar, and the Gurkha, however much he may neglect the remainder of his religious duties, usually contrives to be present at the almost continuous ritual which is carried on during this time.

At sunset on the seventh, or *Phulpati,* day, a big review of the Kathmandu garrison takes place. This is held on the Thuni Khel, the big grass-covered parade ground in the centre of the city. All round the Thuni Khel the people stand in dense masses awaiting the arrival of the King who, on this occasion, makes one of his rare appearances in public. Every one is dressed in gala attire, the bright dresses of the womenfolk adding further touches of colour to the natural brightness of the scene. The troops are drawn up, forming three sides of a square, and the artillery is massed in the space left, with the combined bands of all the regiments in the centre. Near the middle of the parade ground is a large tree, and below this is a platform on which His Majesty, supported by a large gathering of Nepalese nobility, takes his stand. At a given signal all the troops on parade commence to fire a *feu-de-joie,* and in this the artillery presently join. The noise quickly becomes deafening and continues for some twenty minutes, when it suddenly ceases. His Majesty now takes his departure, and the enormous crowd of spectators which throng the edges of the parade ground gradually disperses to continue the festivities in their own homes, while the troops return to their quarters.

At sunset on the next, or *Astami,* day, the actual sacrificial ceremony commences and lasts throughout the night, only terminating at eight or nine the following morning.

On this occasion buffaloes and goats are sacrificed by means of decapitation with a *khukri,* the number thus offered to the goddess Durga being solely dependent on the means of those making the sacrifice. On this day the scene at the Kot, in Kathmandu, where no less than seven regiments are quartered, must be seen to be believed. The helpless animals are dragged into the arena, seemingly aware of their fate, and brought up to the post before which their executioner stands ready to administer the *coup-de-grace.* The decapitation of a fully-grown buffalo at one stroke of the *khukri* is a feat demanding no ordinary strength and skill, and the successful performance of this operation invariably wins the applause of the crowd. Failure to sever the head from the body at one stroke is considered an occurrence of ill omen, and the onlookers are quick to express their disapproval of the performer's lack of skill by smearing his face with the still warm blood of his unfortunate victim. On the other hand, the clean, sure stroke is greeted with applause, and the performer is rewarded with the gift of a new white *pagri* or turban, which is tied round his head by the highest in rank present at the moment.

As the ceremony proceeds, both onlookers and performers become gradually worked up into a religious frenzy, stimulated by the gruesome sights taking place before them. By this time the arena is streaming with blood and the headless carcases of the recently slaughtered victims lie about on all sides. In one corner sits a Brahman, the priest officiating at the ceremony. Only he is imperturbable as he chants incessantly the appropriate verses from the Hindu sacred books. In front of him burns a small lamp; this is the sacred flame, and around it are strewn the petals of the marigold, a flower indispensable for any Hindu religious ceremony. As each animal falls the body is dragged to one side and the dripping head is placed in front of the officiating priest, until finally he is almost obscured from view by the heap of bleeding tokens. The conclusion of the ceremony is marked by the pulling up of the young barley shoots which were planted on the first day. This is carried out by the Brahmans, who distribute small bunches in returns for the gifts which are always offered to them.

A similar ceremony, but naturally on a smaller scale, takes place in every village in Nepal on this occasion, and the festival is also celebrated at the various headquarters of the Gurkha Regiments of the Indian Army.

Twenty days after the conclusion of the Dasehra, the festival known as Diwali takes place. This lasts for five days and is sacred to Lakshmi, the goddess of wealth and prosperity, and the consort of the god Vishnu. According to Hindu mythology, Vishnu is said to have killed at this time of the year Marakasur, a hitherto invincible giant, after a desperate battle, and to have entered his city in triumph early on the following morning. The people illuminated the city and received him with joy, and from this cause the festival is called "The Festival of Illumination," and is kept up to commemorate this great victory of Vishnu.

This festival, whatever its religious significance may formerly have been, is now looked upon as the great opportunity of the year for gambling in public. Throughout Nepal gambling, normally forbidden, is for three days allowed to take place without let or hindrance, and the Gurkha, born gambler as he is, takes full advantage of the opportunity thus offered to indulge in one of his favourite pastimes.

There is no limit to which a Gurkha will not go when in gambling mood, and many are the stories relating to the heavy and curious stakes for which the Nepalese have, on occasion, played. It is stated, for instance, that men have staked their wives on a throw of the dice, and one man is even said to have cut off his left hand and placed it under a cloth as a stake. On finding himself the winner it is related of him that he demanded his opponent's hand, or the refund of the money he had previously lost.

Although gambling plays a very important part in this festival, the five days during which it takes place are dedicated to the worship of certain animals and people, who are looked upon as sacred during this period. There appears to be a slight variation in the objects worshipped, but, generally speaking, a day is devoted to the worship of each of the following : The crow; the dog; the cow; the bull; and the brother; but of these, only the last three appear to be worshipped throughout Nepal.

On the fifth, or last, day the daughters of the household regard their brothers in the light of deities, and the ceremonial on this occasion includes the placing by the sister of the caste mark on her brother's forehead.

During the whole period of Diwali every house is nightly illuminated by as many little lamps as the householders can produce; and in the case of a large city like Kathmandu this illumination is most effective. On every window are to be seen rows of little earthenware lamps, and even the streets are filled with brightly illuminated booths which, on closer inspection, prove to be gambling dens in miniature.

The third, and remaining, major festival celebrated throughout Nepal is that known as the Holi. This is held in honour of the god Krishna, and takes place eight days before the full moon of the month of *Phagun,* or early in March.

The ceremony consists in the erection of a wooden post, or pine tree, decorated with streamers of red-and-white cloth. On the last day of the festival this is burnt with much ceremony, and the rite is believed to represent the burning of the body of the old year.

During these eight days it is the fashion to perambulate the streets armed with a bag of bright-red powder, known as *golal,* with which passers-by are plentifully bombarded. Little regard is paid to the clothes, and towards the latter part of the festival most people exhibit traces of their active participation in it.

In former days this festival was the occasion for much obscene behaviour, but latterly this practice has become modified.

The remaining, purely Hindu, festivals are not of sufficient interest to merit detailed description, but for the benefit of those interested in the subject they are tabulated at the end of the book. Generally speaking they are similar in their detail to those of which a description may be found in the standard works on Hindu customs.

8

THE GOVERNMENT AND ADMINISTRATION OF NEPAL

Nepal enjoys complete political independence, and her relations with the British Government are regulated by the Treaty of Friendship. This was concluded in 1923, and its most important clauses accord to Nepal permission to import arms, ammunition, and other stores from and through British India. Each country has a minister accredited at the Court of the other. On the British side the minister is styled British Envoy at the Court of Nepal, and resides in Kathmandu. The Nepalese representative is accredited to the Government of India, with whom he deals direct.

It can thus be seen that the position of Nepal in no way resembles that of the Native States of India, whose policy is directed by Government, but is rather that of an ally with whom we are on particularly friendly terms.

Under the treaty of A.D. 1856 Nepal receives an annual tribute of ten thousand rupees from Tibet, but except in the way of trade, there is little intercourse between the two countries. A Nepalese representative is in residence

* Northey & Morris.

at Lhasa, the capital of Tibet, but his duties are simply to safeguard the trade interests of his countrymen.

Nepal had, at one time, friendly relations with China, but since the Sino-Tibetan imbroglio the road from China to Nepal has remained blocked, and no effort has been made to reopen political relations with that country.

Landlocked as the country is, its external relations have, up to date, been confined to the above.

His Majesty the Maharajadhiraj, as the King is called, is the sovereign of this independent Hindu kingdom, but His Highness the Maharaja, as the Prime Minister is styled, is the virtual ruler of the country, and is, to all intents and purposes, supreme in all matters affecting government, whether political, administrative, executive, or military. He is advised, in all matters of importance, by ordinary and extraordinary councils, composed of Bharadars, or Nobles, and certain officers of the State, according as the nature and gravity of the matter under consideration may require.

For ordinary administrative purposes the country is divided into circles, each under a separate official known as Bara Hakim, or principal district officer, who is the local representative of the Government in all matters, both civil and military. His position is somewhat analagous to that of a district commissioner in India under the old regime, when civil and military duties were combined under one official.

A circle consists of a number of *jillas* (districts) or *thums*, in the hills, and of two jillas only in the Terai, and at the headquarters of each there are collectorates for revenue and also judicial courts.

The bulk of the revenue of the country is derived from land dues. The average rent per bigha (a measure of land equal to about half an acre) of land in the Terai varies, according to the class of land and locality, from two to nine rupees, and in the hills from a half to one rupee. The reason for the difference in rates is due to the fact that the Terai land is more productive than that in the hills.

Other sources of revenue are customs duty, fines levied at courts of justice, sale of timber, hides and skins. There is, however, no system of direct taxation in Nepal. The total amount of revenue is said, by the Nepal Government, to amount to about one and a half crores of rupees per annum.

For the collection and payment of land revenue each village has an officer known as a *Mukhiya* (head-man). These men collect rent from tenants of Government land and are provided with rent rolls for this purpose, the amounts so Elected being paid into the nearest *jilla*. The Mukhiyas are remunerated with five per cent, of their collections, and are also entitled to one day's service a year from each man m their village. The office is hereditary, but m the event of a vacancy occurring by reason of there being no heir, or of a change necessitated by misconduct, the post is filled either by popular vote or by a nominee of the nearest Government official.

The chief crop of the Terai is rice but oil seed and jute pulse are frequently grown as a second crop. In the lower hills rice, again, is the staple crop, while higher up its place is taken by maize or Indian corn. After these, barley, wheat and millet are the other crops most usually seen.

Copper, iron and lead are to be found in various parts of Nepal, but the mines are worked on primitive lines and no attempt has been made to use modern scientific methods, it being left to the local inhabitants to extract what they can of the minerals on payment of certain royalties to Government.

Explorations made in what were considered promising areas in the Nepal valley have, so far, resulted in the finding of deposits of only lignite coal which, too inferior in quality for domestic purposes, is used only in brick kilns.

Nepal is fortunate in the possession of much valuable forest land, most of which is situated in the Terai area, but it is only of recent years that steps have been taken to exploit this to its fullest extent. Regarded as a timber-producing area, the Terai can be divided into four different forest zones. Firstly, the forests of Sal (*Shorea Robusta*), the most important tree in the country; secondly, the riveraine forests of Shisham (*Dalbergia Sissoo*) and Khair (*Acacia*); thirdly, mixed deciduous forests, in which the predominant trees are Asna (*Terminalia tomentosa*), the Simal (*Bombax Malabaricum*), and the Toon (*Cedrela Toona*); lastly, the moist Savannah forests, consisting of areas of tall grasses.

Above the Terai, in the temperate zone, where live a large part of the population, forest areas may again be divided. Firstly, a belt situated between 4,000 and 8,500 feet above sea-level, containing such trees as oaks, maples and pines; secondly, the forest above 8,500 feet, in which spruces, firs and larches are the chief species. Although the temperate zone is of comparatively little commercial importance, it fulfils a purpose even more important than that of a source of revenue, in that it supplies the dense population of this area with fuel, timber and grazing.

In the Alpine zones we find only the rhododendrons and juniper—trees of no commercial importance, although useful as fuel.

External trade is practically confined to British India. In former times a considerable amount of commerce was carried on with Tibet, but since the opening of the trade route between that country and Kalimpong, in North-Eastern Bengal, it has dwindled to a negligible quantity, and the trade with Tibet now consists mainly of bartering Nepalese foodstuffs and utensils for salt, wool, woollen blankets and sheep. Rice and other food grains, ghi, oil seeds, jute, animals, timber and dye-stuffs are the main constituents of the export trade with British India, piece goods, cotton twist and yarn, metals, spices, salt and sugar of the import trade.

Nepal has its own coinage, which is struck at the Government Mint at Kathmandu. It comprises gold, silver and copper coins, the first-named being used principally as ceremonial gifts. Of the silver coins there are pieces of various value, but those in current use are a rupee and a half-rupee piece, called *mohur*. The Nepali rupee stands at a discount of twenty-five per cent, compared with the rupee of British India. Copper coins are also manufactured at various places in the vicinity of the mines, and this accounts for the very crude appearance and design of many of the examples met with.

Owing to the absence throughout the country of roads, as we know them, the conveyance of mails is no easy problem, and this is carried out entirely by runners. Post offices are few and far between, and posts infrequent. As, however, the bulk of the people are practically illiterate, this is not such a hardship as might otherwise appear.

The laws are based on the Hindu *Shastras*, modified to suit the customs and spirit of the times. They may be roughly divided into civil, revenue and criminal, and do not differ greatly from the code in force in British India. It may be noted, however, that Brahmans and women are exempt from capital punishment, no matter what the nature of their crime. Prisoners undergoing sentence appear to be well cared for, and can often be seen in the streets of Kathmandu, where they are employed on various public works. They are allowed great latitude in the matter of leaving their prisons, and are easily recognizable by the tight-fitting steel bands which are riveted on to either leg.

In Kathmandu there is stationed a considerable police force, conspicuous by their blue cotton uniforms and scarlet *pagris*. Outside the valley of Nepal, the duties of the police are performed, to a great extent, by the soldiers forming the various local garrisons, their duties, in fact, consist of little else.

Nepal is essentially a military country, and the few Europeans who have from time to time been permitted to visit the valley have all remarked on the signs of military dominance met with at every turn. As has been pointed out, the local police work is almost entirely in the hands of the military, and the power thus obtained, together with their military rank, gives them almost complete dominance over the country people. A military party arriving in a small village has only to make known its wants to have them attended to immediately. The position is somewhat analogous to that obtaining in Prussia before the war, save that the soldiery of Nepal cannot be said to be on bad terms with the civil population. The profession of arms has, from time immemorial, been looked upon as the highest to which a man not of noble birth can attain, and it is this fact which is probably responsible for the respect with which members of the military profession are everywhere regarded.

The army, including the irregulars, or militia, stands at a total of slightly over 44,000, on a peace footing; a large percentage for a country whose total population is but five and a half millions.

Recruits are obtained by voluntary enlistment, and in normal circumstances no difficulty is experienced in obtaining the requisite numbers.

The army is drawn from the so-called fighting classes of Nepal. These are all dwellers in the hill country, and consist of Thakurs, Chetris, Gurungs, Magars, Rais, Limbus and Sunwars. In a country where aristocratic birth is considered of paramount importance it naturally follows that the bulk of the army should be composed of the two first-named classes, the Chetris greatly predominating.

The army is divided into 31 regiments, which include

two of artillery, and a regiment of cavalry, consisting of but 120 sabres. These latter are used mostly as orderlies and as outriders in attendance upon members of the royal family.

In the majority of the regiments men of all the above-mentioned classes are to be found serving side by side. There are, however a few regiments whose members consist entirely of one caste. Amongst these latter are the Kali Bahadur and the Kali Parshad Regiments, composed entirely of Gurungs, and the Purana Gorakh, whose ranks are only open to Magars.

The *corps d'elite,* however, is composed of men of all classes, and is known as the Rifle Regiment. The men in it are of magnificent physique, and none of them is less than six feet in height. They are almost entirely employed in guarding the royal person, and may be regarded in a similar light to our own Household Troops.

In addition to the regular army, the greater part of which is permanently stationed in the capital, there is a further body of troops, known as the militia. These are raised locally, and do not usually leave the districts in which they live. They enrol for a period of five years, and are trained for three months every other year.

Until quite recently the army was mostly paid by means of grants of land. Of recent years, however, these land payments have been gradually replaced by monthly payments in cash, and before long the whole army will be paid on this system.

The regulars are armed with short Lee-Enfield and Martini-Henry rifles, together with a few Lewis and machine guns; while the militia have only muskets. The artillery is equipped with light mountain guns, and has in addition a few mortars, or howitzers, of very old pattern. Firearms and ammunition are manufactured at the Government arsenal, but their make and quality are greatly inferior to the modern weapons of precision with which the army is now armed, and which are, in the main, the gift of the British Government.

One curious custom in connection with the army needs to be mentioned. This is the system of service by rotation. Thus, if after a time a man desires to proceed to his home, he first arranges for a friend to take the place he will leave vacant in the regiment. These men, known as Dhakre, after spending a few years at home, may again enter the ranks and take the place of others who, in turn, lie by for a year or two. This system, particularly adapted to the country, affords much scope for the gratification of the Gurkhas' innate yearning for military service, and in addition provides a large body of partially trained men which would be available in any time of emergency.

The regiments stationed at the capital are not provided with quarters, but make their own arrangements. This system, whilst undoubtedly unsatisfactory from many points of view, is well enough adapted to the present needs of the army. It is reasonable to predict, however, that as the country progresses barracks will eventually be provided, and the discipline of the army will, in consequence, improve.

Before the War the whole army was clothed in bright-blue cotton uniform, with a very distinctive headdress, consisting of a kind of skull cap with a tightly rolled brim all round, adorned with silver or brass wire, according to rank, and finished off with the regimental emblem in front. Though still worn in the country districts, this picturesque dress is gradually giving way to the more serviceable khaki.

Although the material of which the Nepalese Army is composed is undoubtedly good, and admirably adapted to the defence of the country, for which it is primarily intended, yet it can in no way be compared with modern regular troops. Perhaps the chief weakness in the army is due to the fact that the majority of its officers are chosen by reason of their social position, rather than for their social position, rather than for their military efficiency; but, even so, the army would undoubtedly constitute a formidable foe if ever called upon to fight in its own hill country.

9

SLAVERY AND THE LABOUR PROBLEM

Amongst the many reforms introduced into the country under the beneficent and farseeing rule of the present Prime Minister, the abolition of slavery occupies a prominent place.

It will come as a surprise to many that until quite recently slavery existed in a nation so fiercely jealous of its own independence as Nepal. Although differing in form to an extent that admitted no comparison with that which prevailed in other countries in bygone days, the fact remains that the system did exist, and the Prime Minister never relaxed his unceasing efforts to abolish an institution which, according to the standards of the civilized world, inflicted a grave stigma on the fair name of Nepal.

It can well be imagined that the introduction of a reform destined to uproot a custom so firmly planted in the social life of the country, and sanctioned by religion, was a matter that called for unusual judgment and discernment. By his tact and personality, however, the

* Northey & Morris.

Prime Minister proved fully equal to handling so difficult a task, and in the winter of 1924 a decree was passed in which the abolition of slavery throughout Nepal was promulgated.

In view of the fact that Nepal was one of the few countries in which this institution existed at so recent a date, we have considered it a matter of interest to describe the form under which slavery existed here, and the events which led up to its gradual limitation and final abolition.

Slavery existed in Nepal from time immemorial, and, indeed, was claimed to be as old as the traditions of the country. It found a mention in the *Smritis* and *Tantras,* ancient books in which, among other things, the whole system of dealing with slaves was expounded and various details regarding their treatment in certain circumstances laid down. The institution of slavery had, in fact, been so fused into the everyday life of the Nepalese that it had gradually become a national custom.

The Government of Nepal had for a long time been considering the best means of ameliorating conditions in an institution os fraught with evil. As far back as 1896 a *Lal Mohur,* or Commission, was promulgated in which all the four *Varnas* or castes were emphatically prohibited from enslaving any free man, woman or child. This decree subsequently became law, and was re-enacted under every successive Government since that date. This was followed by further legislation, which had as its object the amelioration of the condition of the slaves, and included a clause under which offences against slaves were punishable in a like manner to those against free men. With the object of inducing them to settle in such parts of the country as Naya Mulk and Morang, in the Terai, further enactments were introduced exempting runaway slaves who were discovered living in these districts from being captured and restored to their owners. A considerable time elapsed before any improvement was visible in the slaves' condition in spite of the sincere intentions of the Nepal Government, as these decrees were not widely promulgated. With the spread of education, however, and the advent of a more progressive age, knowledge of what constituted their rights could no longer be withheld from the slaves, and it gradually came to be known that a slave who availed himself to the fullest extent of the new legislation became, in everything but name, a free man.

In a population numbering some five and a half millions, the total number of persons affected by the abolition of the system was not very large. According to returns specially prepared the number of slave-owners was 15,719, and those held in slavery 51,419, from which it will be seen that roughly only 1 per cent, of the entire population was concerned. Although the owners, being as a rule possessed of large estates and employing much labour, were, for the most part, men who enjoyed a certain prominence and social status in their own sphere, yet their numerical inferiority rendered the task of abolishing the system easier; pointing, as it did, to the obvious inference that the employment of slaves appeared not only inacceptable, but unnecessary, in the eyes of the bulk of the population.

The men owning slaves could be grouped broadly into three classes. There were those who found themselves the possessors of slaves as the result of the inheritance of a large estate of which they formed part and parcel. To these men the abolition of slavery was hailed with appreciation, for detesting, for the most part, a system under which human beings—in appearance, feelings and sensibilities the same as themselves—had been, by an evil destiny, subjected to the degrading conditions that slavery imposed, they were, in consequence, kindly disposed towards their unfortunate fellow beings, and treated them in a humane manner, often assisting them in the upbringing of their children and in the support of their parents. Next came those owners who maintained slaves purely for labour. Living chiefly in isolated places and depending entirely on their slaves to carry on their household and farm work, it was but natural that these men looked with apprehension on a proposal that appeared to them to threaten their very existence. Lastly, there were those owners, few in number, who maintained slaves in order to carry out a nefarious trade in human beings. These men did not scruple to separate husband from wife, or mother from child. They did not hesitate to resort to any method, however base, to circumvent the law, their only aim and object being to become rich as quickly as possible by the most reprehensible and revolting means.

With the exception of the last-mentioned class, the treatment of slaves, as the ancient statutes had recommended, had always been humane, and it is clear that the cruelty and oppression which existed in other countries where slavery was practised were, to a large extent, lacking in Nepal. Cases were by no means infrequent where slaves who had served long and faithfully in one family took an active interest in its welfare, in some cases even assuming entire control during the minority of an heir. There were households where, during the absence of the master on business or pleasure, the slaves could be trusted to ensure that no dislocation or interruption of the daily routine occurred, while in others the distinction between master and slave was practically non-existent.

Although the slaves' lot was, in many cases, not an unhappy one, yet kind treatment could do but little to mitigate the thought of the hopeless bondage into which they had been born and which branded them with the mark of servitude before all their fellow men. As can be easily realized, it was in the matter of the slaves' marriage and family that many evil practices and abuses of the existing regulations began to creep in, and the exposure of many of the worst cases, opening the eyes of people to the existence of a state of affairs which had been, up to then, a sealed book, doubtless played a large part in winning the support of the country for the Prime Minister in his humane proposals.

Realizing the importance of increasing the supply of labour on their estates, the slave-owners took the earliest opportunities of finding mates for their unfortunate bond servants. Under the laws of the country which obtained prior to the abolition of slavery, the father of a child by a slave girl, if he were a free man other than the owner, could emancipate it by payment of a certain stipulated sum to the master of the girl. Many cases, however, were found to exist where slave girls were given as concubines to men who were in too straitened circumstances to emancipate any offspring that ensued. In cases such as these the children remained the property of the slave-owner, who was at liberty to dispose of them as he pleased. Where the children were the result of union between a slave girl and her owner they were automatically set free under the law. The unscrupulous slave-owner therefore evaded the provisions of the law by handing over his slave women to the embraces of impoverished strangers. It can easily be understood what suffering and hardship ensued in families brought up under these conditions. Cases were bound to occur where the master found himself unable to afford to keep the slave's increasing family, and when this occurred, it was, as might be expected, on the slaves that the burden of additional hardship or separation fell. The natural consequence of such a state of affairs was that no ambition or qualities, such as prudence and thrift, could be expected to take shape in the minds of beings brought up, from their earliest infancy, to regard themselves as mere goods and chattels, and that their normal impulse was to do the least possible amount of work that would ensure them a bare existence.

The evils accruing from such a state of things were clearly recognized by the ruling authorities, and in 1921 a law was passed investing the slaves with the right to own and inherit property. Even this was found to produce little amelioration of the slaves' condition; for owing to the fact that the slaves had little or no time of their own, opportunities for them to earn money were exceedingly limited, and property, in most cases, was confined to personal belongings.

The arguments urged by the slave-owners against the proposals to abolish an institution which formed part of their livelihood were varied. It was urged that in such matters as the guarding of their property a greater reliability could be placed on slaves, as by virtue of their being the personal property of their master they would be easier of arrest should they, by any chance, violate the trust which had been placed in them. Another argument that was frequently produced was that with the abolition of slavery the slaves themselves might leave the country. Fears such as these might, with reason, have been entertained by slave-owners in such countries as the West Indies and Mauritius, where the population, in those days, consisted of aliens forcibly taken away from their homes and retained in bondage. In Zanzibar, when slavery flourished, there were 200,000 slaves to less than 100,000 free men, and in the West Indies again slaves reached a total of 700,000. In countries such as these, where the land under slave cultivation comprised an enormous area, and where such a large number of skilled labourers was difficult to replace, the possibility of a general exodus might, with reason, be regarded with apprehension. In the case of the slaves of Nepal, however, the danger was not apparent, for the majority were born and bred in the country, and their family ties and occupations—involving, generally, employment on domestic and farm work in the home land—were such as to preclude any idea of their leaving the country altogether.

In addition to those provided by slaves, there were other reserves of labour which could be called up at certain seasons of the year when agricultural operations were at their heaviest. Under one of these, a system of co-operative labour, known as Parma, every household furnishes what labour it can in times of transplantation or gathering in of crops, to other households, subsequently receiving similar help in return. Again, in cases where estates are large and many labourers are required, when help available under the Parma system is insufficient, hired labourers, known as Bant or Darmahadars, are often employed. These are engaged for periods of varying duration—on occasions even for a single day—and are provided with food and a small remuneration either in kind or in money. A special feature of this custom is that the contract for service may extend to a month, or to several months, or even to a year, and it may be renewed on expiry. In certain of the hill districts the total monthly expenditure involved under this system was found to work out at about six rupees (nine shillings) per man. Careful inquiries have shown that, given an equal number of slaves and Bant labourers, the output from cultivation worked under the Bant system amounted to nearly twice as much as that worked by slaves, while the expense involved was very little more.

Another argument against the abolition of slavery was that slaves, when well treated, were in a less unfavourable position than the *Bandas*. These are persons who have become hopelessly indebted, or who are compelled by urgent reasons to raise sums of money which they can only repay by their personal labour. The *Banda* will enter into a legal contract to work solely for his creditor until his debt is paid off. Consequently a *Banda* may be in a worse plight than an actual slave, as the creditor has less interest in the *Banda's* physical well-being than a humane slave-owner would have. This, however, is an argument against the *Banda* system rather than a valid point in favour of slavery.

It was not until November 28, 1924, that the Prime Minister, in an eloquent speech at Kathmandu, disclosed the details of his proposals, which were subsequently adopted, for the complete emancipation of slaves and the abolition of slavery. The proposals comprised three main clauses, which were as follows:—

> Firstly, that from a certain date, to be fixed as early as possible, having regard to the state of public opinion, the legal status of slavery should cease throughout Nepal. Secondly, that the owners be paid a statutory price for each slave whose claim had been fully established. Lastly, that the slaves, after receiving their freedom, should be apprenticed to their former owners for a period of seven years, during which time they would have to work for them and would in return be provided with food and clothing. The last clause was introduced in the hope that the freed slaves would, by performing, as free men, the same duties which they had previously carried out as slaves, gradually accustom themselves to the new order of things, and would accordingly eventually settle down as ordinary hired labourers in the localities where they had been living. It was evident that during the process of readjustment the onus of maintaining the old and infirm as well as the very young, which had been borne up to now by the slave-owners, would be transferred to the slaves themselves, and the owners were accordingly asked gradually to substitute wages in kind or money for the food and clothing they had been in the habit of giving, to enable the slaves to bear the burden which the maintenance of their dependants would lay upon them.

Although slavery has been definitely abolished throughout Nepal, there still exists a kind of forced labour, which is divided into three classes, known respectively as *Begari, Thara* and *Beti.* Of these, the first two are in force in order to supply official requirements, and are enforced under the orders of the local authorities, through the village headmen. *Begari* applies solely to questions of transport work, which, owing to the absence of roads passable for vehicles, is performed almost entirely by coolies. This form of labour is put into force on such occasions as the tour of a Governor, or other important official, for the transport of whose baggage a large number of porters may be required.

The second form, *Thara,* is confined to such labour as may be required in connection with the building of bridges and roads, the roofing of houses, and clearing of forests. It may be enforced for a period of several days, and in some cases may even extend to a month.

The last form of forced labour is known as *Bethi.* It consists in the carrying out of work, of a purely private nature, for the headman of a village, such as thatching of a roof or working in the fields, and constitutes part of his pay. Every one is liable for this for one day in the year, and exemption can be obtained on the payment of the small sum of four annas.

Although not strictly speaking a labour question, the method of obtaining Gurkha recruits for the twenty battalions of the Indian Army may perhaps be mentioned here. As has been explained, Nepal is closed to Europeans, so that the recruiting officers are not themselves able to take an active part in the work. The system adopted is for each regiment to send a small party to Gorakhpur in India, and not far from the Nepal frontier. From this place these recruiters are sent out into the Nepalese hills, and return as soon as they have been able to pick up a few likely lads whom they bring in to the recruiting headquarters. This work is only carried on during the winter, as at other times of the year the Terai, through which all must pass on their way to and from the hills, is very unhealthy.

10

GURKHA

Gurkha, also spelled as Gorkha or Ghurka (Nepali: गोर्खा), are people from Nepal who take their name from the 8th century Hindu warrior-saint Guru Gorakhnath. His disciple Bappa Rawal, born *Prince Kalbhoj/Prince Shailadhish,* founded the house of Mewar, Rajasthan (Rajputana). Later descendants of Bappa Rawal moved further east to found the house of Gorkha, which in turn founded the Kingdom ofNegal. Gorkha District is one of the 75 districts of modern Nepal.

Gurkhas are best known for their history of bravery and strength in the Indian Army's Gorkha regiments and the British Army's Brigade of Gurkhas. The Gurkhas were designated by British officials as a "Martial Race". "Martial Race" was a designation created by officials of British India to describe "races" (peoples) that were thought to be naturally warlike and aggressive in battle, and to possess qualities of courage, loyalty, self sufficiency, physical strength, resilience, orderliness, the ability to work hard for long periods of time, fighting tenacity and military strategy. The British recruited heavily from these Martial Races for service in the British Indian Army.

Former Chief of staff of the Indian Army, Field Marshal Sam Manekshaw once famously said about Gurkhas:

> "If a man says he is not afraid of dying, he is either lying or is a Gurkha."

Etymology

The word Gorkha is derived from the Prakrit words "gao rakkha" (Sanskrit *gau-raksa,* literally "cow-protector"). This was used by Guru Gorakhnath, the spiritual leader of the Gorkhas. the name given to his disciples.

History

Gurkhas claim descent from the Hindu Rajputs of Northern India who entered modern Nepal from the west. Guru Gorkhanath had a Rajput Prince-disciple, the legendary Bappa Rawal, born *Prince Kalbhoj/Prince Shailadhish,* founder of the Royal house of Mewar, who became the first Gurkha and is said to be the ancestor of the Royal family of Nepal. Historian G. L. Rai however says that they are not related to Rajputs.

The majority of the early Gurkhas were from the Thakuri/Rajput (which includes the Shah dynasty and Rana dynasty of Nepal), Chetri and Brahmin ethnic groups, whereas the modern Gurkha soldiers are also from the Limbu, Rai, Gurung and Magar ethnic groups. They joined the Gurkhas during 17th century expansion of the Gurkha kingdom. However, even today the Thakuris and Chetris make up the majority of Gurkha officers in Nepal, while the Gurkha army also have Limbu, Rai, Gurung and Magar people, this combination of warriors from different ethnic groups made the Gurkhas a dominant military force in the history of the Indian subcontinent since the 18th century.

The legend states that Bappa Rawal was a teenager in hiding, when he came upon the warrior saint while on a hunting expedition with friends in the jungles of

Rajasthan. Bappa Rawal chose to stay behind, and care for the warrior saint, who was in deep meditation. When Guru Gorkhanath awoke, he was pleased with the devotion of Bappa Rawal. The Guru gave him the *Kukri (Khukuri) knife,* the famous curved blade of the present day Gurkhas. The legend continues that he told Bappa that he and his people would henceforth be called Gurkhas, the disciples of the Guru Gorkhanath, and their bravery would become world famous. He then instructed Bappa Rawal, and his Gurkhas to stop the advance of the Muslims, who were invading *Afghanistan* (which at that time was a Hindu/Buddhist nation). Bappa Rawal took his Gurkhas and liberated Afghanistan—originally named Gandhara, from which the present day Kandahar derives its name. He and his Gurkhas stopped the initial Islamic advance of the 8th century in the Indian subcontinent.

There are legends that Bappa Rawal (Kalbhoj) went further conquering Iran and Iraq before he retired as an ascetic at the feet of Mt. Meru, having conquered all invaders and enemies of his faith.

It is a misconception that the Gurkhas took their name from the Gorkha region of Nepal. The region was given its name after the Gurkhas had established their control of these areas. In the early 16th century some of Bappa Rawal's descendants went further east, and conquered a small state in present-day Nepal, which they named Gorkha in honour of their patron saint. By 1769, through the leadership of Sri Panch (5) Maharaj Dhiraj Prithvi Narayan Shahdev (1769-1775), the Gorkha dynasty had taken over the area of modern Nepal. They made Hinduism the state religion, although with distinct Rajput warrior and Gorkhanath influences.

In the Gurkha War (1814-1816) they waged war against the British East India Company army. The British were impressed by the Gurkha soldiers and after reaching a stalemate with the Gurkhas made Nepal a protectorate. Much later, they were granted the right to freely hire them as mercenaries from the interior of Nepal (as opposed to the early British Gurkha mercenaries who were hired from areas such as Assam (i.e., the Sirmoor Rifles) and were then organised in Gurkha regiments in the East India Company army with the permission of then prime minister, Shree Teen (3) Maharaja (Maharana) Jung Bahadur Rana, the first Rana Prime-minister who initiated a Rana oligarchic rule in Nepal. Jung Bahadur was the grandson of the famous Nepalese hero and Prime minister Bhimsen Thapa. Originally Jung Bahadur and his brother Ranodip Singh brought a lot of modernisation to Nepalese society, the abolition of slavery, undermining of taboos regarding the untouchable class, public access to education, etc. But these dreams were short lived when in the coup d'etat of 1885 the nephews of Jung Bahadur and Ranodip Singh (the Shumshers J.B., S.J.B. or Satra (17) Family) murdered Ranodip Singh and the sons of Jung Bahadur, stole the name of Jung Bahadur and took control of Nepal. This "Shumsher" Rana rule is regarded by some as one of the reasons for Nepal lagging behind in modern development. The children of Jung Bahadur and Ranodip Singh lived mainly outside of Kathmandu, in Nepal, and in India after escaping the coup d'etat of 1885.

The "original" Gurkhas who were descended from the Rajputs (Thakuri and Chetri) refused to enter as soldiers and were instead given positions as officers in the British-Indian armed forces. The non-Kashaktriya Gurkhas entered as soldiers (i.e., Magar, Gurung). The Thakur/Rajput Gurkhas were entered as officers, one of whom, (retired) General Narendra Bahadur Singh, Gurkha Rifles, great grandson of Jung Bahadur, while a young captain, rose to become aide-de-camp (A.D.C.) to Lord Mountbatten of Burma, the last Viceroy of India.

The Gurkha soldier recruits were mainly drawn from several ethnic groups. When the British began recruiting from the interior of Nepal these soldiers were mainly drawn from *Magar, Gurung, Rai and Limbu,* although earlier

British Gurkhas included Garhwalis, Kumaonis, Assamese and others as well.

After the British left India, Gorkhalis continued seeking employment in British and Indian forces, as officers and soldiers. Under international law, present-day British Gurkhas are not treated as mercenaries but are fully integrated soldiers of the British Army, operate in formed units of the Brigade of Gurkhas, and abide by the rules and regulations under which all British soldiers serve.

The Gurkha war cry is "Jai Mahakali, Ayo Gorkhali" which literally translates to "Glory be to the Goddess of War, here come the Gorkhas!"

Professor Sir Ralph Turner, MC, who served with the 3rd Queen Alexandra's Own Gurkha Rifles in the First World War, wrote of Gurkhas:

> "As I write these last words, my thoughts return to you who were my comrades, the stubborn and indomitable peasants of Nepal. Once more I hear the laughter with which you greeted every hardship. Once more I see you in your bivouacs or about your fires, on forced march or in the trenches, now shivering with wet and cold, now scorched by a pitiless and burning sun. Uncomplaining you endure hunger and thirst and wounds; and at the last your unwavering lines disappear into the smoke and wrath of battle. Bravest of the brave, most generous of the generous, never had country more faithful friends than you."

British East India Company Army

Gurkhas served as troops under contract to the East India Company in the Pindaree War of 1817, in Bharatpur in 1826 and the First and Second Anglo-Sikh Wars in 1846 and 1848.

During the Indian Rebellion of 1857, Gurkhas fought

on the British side, and became part of the British Indian Army on its formation. The 8th (Sirmoor) Local Battalion made a particularly notable contribution during the conflict, and indeed twenty-five Indian Order of Merit awards were made to men from that regiment during the Siege of Delhi. Three days after the mutiny began, the Sirmoor Battalion were ordered to move to Meerut, where the British garrison was barely holding on, and in doing so they had to march up to 48 kilometres a day. Later, during the four month Siege of Delhi they defended Hindu Rao's house, losing 327 out of 490 men. During this action they fought side by side with the 60th Rifles and a strong bond developed. Twelve regiments from the Nepalese Army also took part in the relief of Lucknow under the command of Shri Teen (3) Maharaja Maharana Jung Bahadur of Nepal and his older brother C-in-C Ranaudip Singh (Ranodip or Ranodeep) Bahadur Rana (later to succeed Jung Bahadur and become Sri Teen Maharaja Ranodip Singh of Nepal).

After the rebellion the 60th Rifles pressed for the Sirmoor Battalion to become a rifle regiment. This honour was granted then next year (1858) when the Battalion was renamed the Sirmoor Rifle Regiment and awarded a third colour. In 1863 Queen Victoria presented the regiment with the Queen's Truncheon, as a replacement for the colours that rifle regiments do not usually have.

British Indian Army (c. 1857-1947)

From the end of the Indian Rebellion of 1857 until the start of the First World War the Gurkha Regiments saw active service in Burma, Afghanistan, the North-East Frontier and the North-West Frontiers of India, Malta (the Russo-Turkish War, 1877 78), Cyprus, Malaya, China (the Boxer Rebellion of 1900) and Tibet (Younghusband's Expedition of 1905).

Between 1901 and 1906, the Gurkha regiments were renumbered from the 1st to the 10th and redesignated as the Gurkha Rifles. In this time, the Brigade of Gurkhas, as the regiments came to be collectively known, was expanded to twenty battalions within the ten regiments.

During World War I (1914-18), more than 200,000 Gurkhas served in the British Army, suffering approximately 20,000 casualties, and receiving almost 2,000 gallantry awards. The number of Gurkha battalions was increased to thirty-three, and Gurkha units were placed at the disposal of the British high command by the Nepalese government for service on all fronts. Many Nepalese volunteers served in noncombat roles, serving in units such as the Army Bearer Corps and the labour battalions, but there were also large numbers that served in combat in France, Turkey, Palestine, and Mesopotamia. They served on the battlefields of France in the Loos, Givenchy, Neuve Chapelle and Ypres; in Mesopotamia, Persia, Suez Canal and Palestine against Turkish advance, Gallipoli and Salonika. One detachment served with Lawrence of Arabia, while during the Battle of Loos (June-December 1915) a battalion of the 8th Gurkhas fought to the last man, hurling themselves time after time against the weight of the German defences, and in the words of the Indian Corps commander, Lieutenant-General Sir James Willcocks, "... found its Valhalla". During the ultimately unsuccessful Gallipoli campaign in 1915, the Gurkhas were among the first to arrive and the last to leave. The 1st/6th Gurkhas, having landed at Cape Helles, led the assault during the first major operation to take out a Turkish high point, and in doing so captured a feature that later became known as "Gurkha Bluff". At Sari Bair they were the only troops in the whole campaign to reach and hold the crest line and look down on the Straits, which was the ultimate objective. The 2nd Battalion of the 3rd Gurkha Rifles (2nd/3rd Gurkha Rifles) was involved in the conquest of Baghdad.

Following the end of the war, the Gurkhas were returned to India and during the interwar years, they were largely kept away from the internal strife and urban conflicts of the subcontinent, instead being employed largely on the frontiers and in the hills where fiercely independent tribesmen were a constant source of troubles. As such, between the World Wars, the Gurkha regiments fought in the Third Afghan War in 1919 and then participated in numerous campaigns on the North-West Frontier, mainly in Waziristan, where they were employed as garrison troops defending the frontier, keeping the peace amongst the local populace and keeping the lawless and often openly hostile Pathan tribesmen in check. During this time the North-West Frontier was the scene of considerable political and civil unrest and the troops stationed at Razmak, Bannu and Wanna saw an extensive amount of action.

During World War II (1939-45), there were ten Gurkha regiments, with two battalions each making a total of twenty pre-war battalions. Following the evacuation of the BEF from Dunkirk in 1940, the Nepalese government offered to increase recruitment to increase the total number of Gurkha battalions in British service to thirty-five. This would eventually rise to forty-five battalions and in order to achieve this, third and fourth battalions were raised for all ten regiments, with fifth battalions also being raised for 1 GR, 2 GR and 9 GR. This expansion required ten training centres to be established for basic training and regimental records across India. In addition five training battalions were raised, while other units were raised as garrison battalions for keeping the peace in India and defending rear areas. Large numbers of Gurkha men were also recruited for non-Gurkha units, and other specialised functions such as paratroops, signals, engineers, and military police.

A total of 250, 280 Gurkhas served during the war, in almost all theatres. In addition to keeping peace in India, Gurkhas fought in Syria, North Africa, Italy, Greece and against the Japanese in the jungles of Burma, northeast India and also Singapore. They did so with considerable distinction, earning 2,734 bravery awards in the process and suffering around 32,000 casualties in all theatres.

Gurkha Military Rank System in the British Indian Army

Gurkha ranks in the British Indian Army followed the same pattern as those used throughout the rest of the Indian Army at that time. As in the British Army itself, there were three distinct levels: private soldiers, non-commissioned officers and commissioned officers. Commissioned officers within the Gurkha regiments held a Viceroy's Commission, which was distinct from the King's or Queen's Commission that British officers serving with a Gurkha regiment held. Any Gurkha holding a commission was technically subordinate to any British officer, regardless of rank.

British Indian Army and Current Indian Army Ranks/ current British Army Equivalents

Viceroy Commissioned Officers (VCOs) up to 1947 and Junior Commissioned Officers (JCOs) from 1947

- Subedar Major/No equivalent
- Subedar/No equivalent
- Jemadar (now Naib Subedar)/No equivalent

Warrant officers

- Regimental Havildar Major/Regimental Sergeant Major
- Company Havildar Major/Company Sergeant Major

Non-commissioned officers

- Company Quartermaster Havildar/Company Quartermaster Sergeant
- Havildar/Sergeant
- Naik/Corporal

- Lance Naik/Lance Corporal

Private soldiers

- Rifleman

(Source: Cross & Gurung 2002, pp. 33-34).

Notes

- British Army officers received Queen's or King's Commissions, but Gurkha officers in this system received the Viceroy's Commission. After Indian independence in 1947, Gurkha officers in regiments which became part of the British Army received the King's (later Queen's) Gurkha Commission, and were known as King's/Queen's Gurkha Officers (KGO/QGO). Gurkha officers had no authority to command troops of British regiments. The QGO Commission was abolished in 2007.
- Jemadars and subedars normally served as platoon commanders and company 2ICs, but were junior to all British officers, while the subedar major was the Commanding Officer's 'advisor' on the men and their welfare. For a long time it was impossible for Gurkhas to progress further, except that an honorary lieutenancy or captaincy was very rarely bestowed upon a Gurkha on retirement.
- The equivalent ranks in the post-1947 Indian Army were (and are) known as Junior Commissioned Officers (JCOs). They retained the traditional rank titles used in the British Indian Army—Jemadar (later Naib Subedar), Subedar and Subedar Major.
- While in principle any British subject may apply for a commission without having served in the ranks, Gurkhas cannot. It was customary for a Gurkha soldier to rise through the ranks and prove his ability before his regiment would consider offering him a commission.
- From the 1920s Gurkhas could also receive King's Indian Commissions, and later full King's or

Queen's Commissions, which put them on a par with British officers. This was rare until after the Second World War.

- Gurkha officers commissioned from the Royal Military Academy - Sandhurst and Short Service Officers regularly fill appointments up to the rank of major. At least two Gurkhas have been promoted to lieutenant colonel and there is theoretically now no bar to further progression.
- After 1948 the Brigade of Gurkhas (part of the British Army) was formed and adopted standard British Army rank structure and nomenclature, except for the three Viceroy Commission ranks between Warrant Officer 1 and Second Lieutenant—jemadar, subedar and subedar major—which remained, albeit with different rank titles Lieutenant (Queens Gurkha Officer), Captain (QGO) and Major (QGO). The QGO commission was abolished in 2007, Gurkha soldiers are currently commissioned as Late Entry Officers.(as above).

Regiments of the Gurkha Rifles (c.1815-1947)

Memorial of 10th Princess Mary's Own Gurkha Rifles, Winchester Cathedral Hampshire

- 1st King George V's Own Gurkha Rifles (The Malaun Regiment) (raised 1815, allocated to Indian Army at independence in 1947)
- 2nd King Edward VII's Own Gurkha Rifles (The Sirmoor Rifles) (raised 1815, allocated to British Army in 1948)
- 3rd Queen Alexandra's Own Gurkha Rifles (raised 1815, allocated to Indian Army at independence in 1947)
- 4th Prince of Wales's Own Gurkha Rifles (raised

1857, allocated to Indian Army at independence in 1947)

- 5th Royal Gurkha Rifles (Frontier Force) (raised 1858, allocated to Indian Army at independence in 1947)
- 6th Gurkha Rifles, renamed 6th Queen Elizabeth's Own Gurkha Rifles in 1959 (raised 1817, allocated to British Army in 1948)
- 7th Gurkha Rifles, renamed 7th Duke of Edinburgh's Own Gurkha Rifles in 1959 (raised 1902, allocated to British Army in 1948)
- 8th giurkha Rifles (raised 1824, allocated to Indian Army at independence in 1947)
- 9th Gurkha Rifles (raised 1817, allocated to Indian Army at independence in 1947)
- 10th Princess Mary's Own Gurkha Rifles (raised 1890, allocated to British Army in 1948)
- 11th Gorkha Rifles (1918-1922; raised again by India following independence in 1947)
- 25th Gurkha Rifles (1942-1946)
- 26th Gurkha Rifles (1943-1946)
- 29th Gurkha Rifles (1943-1946)
- 42nd Gurkha Rifles (raised 1817 as the Cuttack Legion, renamed 6th Gurkha Rifles in 1903)
- 44th Gurkha Rifles (raised 1824 as the 16th (Sylhet) Local Battalion, renamed 8th Gorkha Rifles in 1903)

Second World War Training Battalions

- 14th Gurkha Rifles Training Battalion
- 38th Gurkha Rifles Training Battalion
- 56th Gurkha Rifles Training Battalion
- 710th Gurkha Rifles Training Battalion

Post-independence (1947-present)

After Indian independence—and partition—in 1947 and under the Tripartite Agreement, the original ten Gurkha regiments consisting of the twenty pre-war battalions were split between the British Army and the newly independent Indian Army. Six Gurkha regiments (twelve battalions) were transferred to the post-independence Indian Army, while four regiments (eight battalions) were transferred to the British Army.

To the disappointment of their British officers the majority of Gurkhas given a choice between British or Indian Army service opted for the latter. The reason appears to have been the pragmatic one that the Gurkha regiments of the Indian Army would continue to serve in their existing roles in familiar territory and under terms and conditions that were well established. The only substantial change was the substitution of Indian officers for British. By contrast the four regiments selected for British service faced an uncertain future in (initially) Malaya—a region where relatively few Gurkhas had previously served. The four regiments (or eight battalions) in British service have since been reduced to a single (two battalion) regiment while the Indian units have been expanded beyond their pre-Independence establishment of twelve battalions.

The principal aim of the Tripartite Agreement was to ensure that Gurkhas serving under the Crown would be paid on the same scale as those serving in the new Indian Army. This was significantly lower than the standard British rates of pay. While the difference is made up through cost of living and location allowances during a Gurkha's actual period of service, the pension payable on his return to Nepal is much lower than would be the case for his British counterparts.

With the abolition of the Nepalese monarchy, the future recruitment of Gurkhas for British and Indian service has been put into doubt. A spokesperson for the

Communist Party of Nepal (Maoist), which is expected to play a major role in the new secular republic, has stated that recruitment as mercenaries is degrading to the Nepalese people and will be banned.

British Army Gurkhas

Four Gurkha regiments joined the British Army on January 1, 1948:

- 2nd King Edward VII's Own Gurkha Rifles (The Sirmoor Rifles)
- 6th Queen Elizabeth's Own Gurkha Rifles
- 7th Duke of Edinburgh's Own Gurkha Rifles
- 10th Princess Mary's Own Gurkha Rifles

They formed the *Brigade of Gurkhas* and were initially stationed in Malaya. There were also a number of additional Gurkha regiments including the 69th Gurkha Field Squadron and the 70th Gurkha Field Support Squadron, both of which were included in the 36th Engineer Regiment. Since then, British Gurkhas have served in Borneo during the Confrontation with Indonesia, in the Falklands conflict, and on various peacekeeping missions in Sierra Leone, East Timor, Bosnia and Kosovo. They are currently serving in Afghanistan.

As of November 2006, the "Brigade of Gurkhas" in the British Army has the following units:

- 1st Battalion, The Royal Gurkha Rifles (1RGR)
- 2nd Battalion, The Royal Gurkha Rifles (2RGR)
- Queen's Gurkha Signals which includes:

  250 Gurkha Signal Squadron

  246 Gurkha Signal Squadron

  248 Gurkha Signal Squadron
- Queen's Own Gurkha Logistics Regiment
- Queen's Gurkha Engineers which includes:

69th Gurkha Field Squadron

70th Gurkha Field Squadron

In addition to these Regiments, the Brigade of Gurkhas has its own clerks and chefs who are posted among the above mentioned units.

Gurkhas in Hong Kong:

- 26th Gurkha Brigade (1948-1950)
- 51st Infantry Brigade (disbanded 1976)
- 48th Gurkha Infantry Brigade (1957-1976; renamed Gurkha Field Force 1976-97; returned to old title 1987-ca.1992)

Indian Army Gorkhas

Upon independence in 1947, six of the original ten Gurkha regiments remained with the Indian Army. These regiments were:

1 Gorkha Rifles

3 Gorkha Rifles

4 Gorkha Rifles

5 Gorkha Rifles

8 Gorkha Rifles

9 Gorkha Rifles

Additionally, a further regiment, 11 Gorkha Rifles, was raised. In 1949 the spelling was changed from "Gurkha" to "Gorkha". All royal titles were dropped when India became a republic in 1950.

Since partition, the Gurkha regiments that were transferred to the Indian Army have established themselves as a permanent and vital part of the newly independent Indian Army. Indeed, while Britain has reduced its Gurkha contingent, India has continued to recruit Gurkhas in large numbers. Indeed, in 2009 the Indian Army had a Gurkha contingent that numbered around 42,000 men in forty-six battalions, spread across seven regiments.

Although their deployment is still governed by the 1947 Tripartite Agreement, in the post-1947 conflicts India has fought in, Gurkhas have served in almost all of them, including the wars with Pakistan in 1947, 1965 and 1971 and also against China in 1962. They have also been used in peacekeeping operations around the world. They have also served in Sri Lanka conducting operations against the Tamil Tigers.

Nepalese Army Gurkhas

Two light infantry battalions of the Nepalese Army are also manned by Gurkhas;

- Shree Purano Gorakh Battalion—established 1763
- Shree Naya Gorakh Battalion—established 1783

These are the oldest Gurkha units in existence, and were utilised as palace guards by the King of Nepal, with one battalion always permanently deployed. The Shree Purano Gorakh Battalion was the first major Nepalese contingent deployed on UN Peacekeeping operations, when it was deployed to the Sinai Peninsula in 1974.

Singapore Gurkha Contingent

The Gurkha Contingent (GC) of the Singapore Police Force was formed on 9 April 1949 from selected ex-British Army Gurkhas. It is an integral part of the Police Force and was raised to replace a Sikh unit which had existed prior to the Japanese occupation during the Second World War.

The GC is a well trained, dedicated and disciplined body whose principal role is as a specialist guard force. In times of crisis it can be deployed as a reaction force. During the turbulent years before and after independence, the GC acquitted itself well on a number of times during outbreaks of civil disorder. The Gurkhas displayed the courage, self restraint and professionalism for which they are famous and earned the respect of the society at large.

Recently the GC can be seen patrolling the streets and have replaced local policemen to guard key installations. The most recent deployment of the GC was to provide additional security for the Singapore Airshow, Asia's largest airshow, and the hunt for the escaped terrorist, Mas Selamat.

Brunei Gurkha Reserve Unit

The Gurkha Reserve Unit is a special guard force in the Sultanate of Brunei. The 2,000 strong Gurkha unit is made up of British Army veterans.

Other

Ethnic identity

Ethnically, Gurkhas who are presently serving in the British armed forces are primarily Indo-Tibeto-Mongolians. Gurkhas serving in the Indian Armed Forces are of both groups, Indo-Tibeto-Mongolian and ethnic Rajput. Gurkhas of Tibeto-Mongolian origin mostly belong to the Rai, Limbu, Gumng, Magar, Tamang, and Kiranti origin Gurkhas are mainly Hindu. The Gurkhas made Hinduism the state religion of Nepal. Very few but some of them are adherents of Tibetan Buddhism and Shamanism, under Hindu influence.

All Gurkhas, regardless of ethnic origin, speak Nepali, also known as Khas Kura or Khas Bhasa, an Indo-Aryan language. They are also famous for their large knife called the khukuri, wtfich is featured in an X shaped configuration on their emblem.

In the mid-1980s some Nepali speaking groups in West Bengal began to organize under the Gorkhaland National Liberation Front, calling for their own Gurkha state, Gorkhaland.

In the introduction to the book Gorkhas Imagined (2009) Prem Poddar makes an important point about the Gorkhas in Nepal versus the Gorkhas in India: "the word 'Gorkha' (or the neologism 'Gorkhaness') as a self-descriptive term ... has gained currency as a marker of difference for Nepalis living in India as opposed to their brethren and sistren in Nepal. Gorkhaliness then becomes synonymous with Indian Nepaleseness but invests only degrees of differential commonalities with Nepali Nepaliness and diasporic Nepaliness. While this counters the irredentism of a Greater Nepal thesis, it cannot completely exorcise the spectres or temptations of an ethnic absolutism for diasporic subjects."

Victoria Cross Recipients

There have been twenty-six Victoria Crosses awarded to members of the Gurkha regiments. The first was awarded in 1858 and the last in 1965. Thirteen of the recipients have been British officers serving with Gurkha regiments, although since 1915 the majority have been received by Gurkhas serving in the ranks as private soldiers or as NCOs. In addition, since Indian independence in 1947, Gurkhas serving in the Indian Army have also been awarded three Param Vir Chakras, which are roughly equivalent.

Of note also, there have been two George Cross medals awarded to Gurkha soldiers, for acts of bravery in situations that have not involved combat.

Treatment of Gurkhas in the United Kingdom

The treatment of Gurkhas and their families was the subject of controversy in the United Kingdom once it became widely known that Gurkhas received smaller pensions than their British counterparts. The nationality status of Gurkhas and their families was also an area of dispute, with claims that some ex-army Nepali families were being denied residency and forced to leave Britain.

On 8 March 2007, the British Government announced that all Gurkhas who signed up after 1 July 1997 would receive a pension equivalent to that of their British counterparts. In addition, Gurkhas would, for the first time, be able to transfer to another army unit after five years' service and women would also be allowed to join - although not in first-line units - conforming to the British Army's policy. The act also guaranteed residency rights in Britain for retired Gurkhas and their families.

Despite the changes, many Gurkhas who had not served long enough to entitle them to a pension faced hardship on their return to Nepal, and some critics derided the Government's decision to only award the new pension and citizenship entitlement to those joining after 1 July 1997, claiming that this left many ex-Gurkha servicemen still facing a financially uncertain retirement. A pressure group, Gurkha Justice Campaign, and the British National Party waded into the debate in support of the Gurkhas.

'In a landmark ruling on 30 September 2008 the High Court in London decided that Gurkhas who left the Army before 1997 did have an automatic right of residency in the United Kingdom. In line with the ruling of the High Court the Home Office is to review all cases affected by this decision.

On the 29 April 2009 a motion in the House of Commons by the Liberal Democrats that all Gurkhas be offered an equal right of residence resulted in a defeat for the Government by 267 votes to 246, the first, first day motion defeat for a government since 1978. Nick Clegg, the Liberal Democrat leader, stated that "This is an immense victory [...] for the rights of Gurkhas who have been waiting so long for justice, a victory for Parliament, a victory for decency." He added that it was "the kind of thing people want this country to do."

On 21 May 2009, the Home Secretary Jacqui Smith announced that all Gurkha veterans who retired before 1997 with at least four years service would be allowed to settle in the UK. The actress and daughter of Gurkha corps major James Lumley, Joanna Lumley, who had highlighted the treatment of the Gurkhas and campaigned for their rights, commented: "This is the welcome we have always longed to give".

A charity, the Gurkha Welfare Trust, provides aid to alleviate hardship and distress among Gurkha ex-servicemen.

Hong Kong

A consisderable number of ex-Gurkhas and their families live in Hong Kong, where they are particularly well represented in the private security profession (G4S Gurkha Services, Pacific Crown Security Service, Sunkoshi Gurkha Security) and among labourers. Ex-Gurkhas left barracks and moved into surrounding urban area. There are considerable Nepalese communities in Yuen Long and Kwun Chung.

British Citizenship

A recent High Court decision on a test case in London has acknowledged the 'debt of honour' to Gurkhas discharged before 1997, and that immigration cases be reviewed, which could set a precedent for citizenship privileges.

Malaysian Armed Forces and Citizenship

After the Federation of Malaya became independent from the United Kingdom in August 1957, many Gurkhas became soldiers in the Malayan armed forces, especially in the Royal Ranger Regiment. Others became security guards, mainly in Kuala Lumpur.

United States Navy

The United States Navy employs Gurkha guards as sentries at its base in Naval Support Activity Bahrain and on the US Navy side of the pier at Mina Salaman. The Gurkhas work alongside Navy members in day-to-day operations.

Popular Culture

- In the video game *Dynasty General,* Gurkha units can be recruited.
- In the video game *Empire: Total War,* the Gurkha unit appears as a special unit.
- In the video game *Age of Empires III: The Asian Dynasties,* Gurkhas appear as long-range riflemen available for the Indian civilization.
- In Michael Crichton's novel *State of Fear* the side hero is a Gurkha.
- In Karen Traviss's novel *Gears of War: Aspho Fields* the Pesang fictional people are heavily based on the Gurkha.
- In the Chris Bunch/Allan Cole The Sten Chronicles series of science fiction novels the Eternal Emperor has a battalion of Gurkha bodyguards recruited from Earth. The bodyguard disbands when the Emperor "dies" and re-enlists when he is "reborn".
- In the song "Funky Days" British band Cornershop mentions, "Before the Gurkhas get called up again...."
- In the Ultimate Force episode "Deadlier Than The Male" the leader of the hijackers, is Captain Allan Eastwood, formerly of the Ghurkas.
- Gurkha is used for the name of United States navy ship, USS Gurkha (SP-600).

INDIAN GORKHA

Indian Gorkha is a term used to describe the Nepali/ Gorkhali-speaking people of India. This term tries to make a distinction between the citizens of Nepal and the Indian citizens of Gorkha ethnic group.

In the introduction to the book Gorkhas Imagined (2009) Prem Poddar makes an important point about the Gorkhas in Nepal versus the Gorkhas in India: "the word 'Gorkha' (or the neologism 'Gorkhaness') as a self-descriptive term ... has gained currency as a marker of difference for Nepalis living in India as opposed to their brethren and sistren in Nepal. Gorkhaliness then becomes synonymous with Indian Nepaleseness but invests only degrees of differential commonalities with Nepali Nepaliness and diasporic Nepaliness. While this counters the irredentism of a Greater Nepal thesis, it cannot completely exorcise the spectres or temptations of an ethnic absolutism for diasporic subjects."

Demographics

It is estimated that there are about 10,000,000 Gorkhas in India but a true count will be possible after the India Census (2011) that is enumerating castes for the first time. In the Darjeeling district of West Bengal there is an estimated 900,000 Gorkhas. The Jalpaiguri district of West Bengal has about 400,000 Gorkhas. There are an estimated 500,000 Gorkhas in Sikkim. In North-East India (states of Assam, Meghalaya, Nagaland, Manipur, Tripura, Mizoram and Arunachal Pradesh), there are several million Gorkhas. A considerable number of Gorkhas also live in the north Indian states of Himachal Pradesh, Uttarakhand and Uttar Pradesh. Gorkhas also live in many Indian cities such as Kolkata, Delhi, Bangalore, Chennai, Mumbai and Hyderabad.

GORKHA DISTRICT

Gorkha District (Nepali: गोर्खा), a part of Gandaki Zone, is one of the seventy-five districts of Nepal, a landlocked country of South Asia. The district, with Pokharithok, later known as Prithivi Narayan Nagarpalika as its district headquarters, covers an area of 3,610km^2 and has a population (2001) of 288,134. It is the location of the Manakamana Temple. Also, the temples of great sage Gorakh Nath and goddess Gorakh Kali temple is located in district, after which the district got its name. Four major rivers run within and along it, they are Chepe, Daraudi, Marsyangdi and Budhi Gandaki.

GORKHA REGIMENTS (INDIA)

Gorkha regiments have been serving in the Indian Army ever since independence in 1947, when the Tripartite Agreement was signed. The regiment primarily consists of soldiers from India's Gorkha community, the regiments have served gallantly under the Indian Army. Composed primarily of Nepalese soldiers, the regiments are famous for their use of the Khukri.

Origins

Impressed by the fighting qualities displayed by the Gorkhas during the Gurkha War, Sir David Ochterlony was quick to realise the potential of the Gorkhas in the British Indian Army. Until then, Gorkha defectors were generally used as irregular forces. In April 1815, the first battalion of the Gorkha Regiment, was raised as the Nasiri regiment. This regiment later became the 1st King George's Own Gurkha Rifles, and saw action at the Maulun fort under Lieutenant Lawtie.

They were instrumental in the expansion of the British East India Company throughout the subcontinent. The Gorkhas took part in the Anglo-Sikh wars, Afghan wars, and in suppressing the Indian Rebellion of 1857. Throughout these years, the British continued to recruit the Gorkhas and kept increasing the number of Gorkha regiments.

By the time First World War started, there were 11 Gorkha regiments under the British Indian Army. The Gorkha regiments played a vital role in the

Commonwealth armies during both the World Wars seeing action everywhere from Monte Cassino in the west to Rangoon in the east, earning Battle Honours everywhere. As a testament to the psychological factors of the Gorkha Regiments on its enemies, during the North African campaign, the German Afrika Corp accorded great respect to the brave khukris wielding Gorkhas.

Post Independence

Following India's independence, India, Nepal and Great Britain signed a Tripartite Agreement, and six regiments of the Gurkha Rifles joined the Indian Army. In 1950, when India became a republic, the Royal titles were dropped from the regiments that joined the Indian Army.

Following the divisions of the Gorkha regiments, the British Army decided that joining of the British Army would be entirely voluntary for the Gorkha soldiers and decided to hold a referendum. As a result, large numbers of men from the 7th Gurkha Rifles and the 10th Gurkha Rifles, which recruited predominantly from Eastern Nepal, decided not to join their regiments as part of the British Army. In order to retain a contingent from this area of Nepal, the Indian Army made the decision to re-raise the 11 Gorkha Rifles, which was disbanded after 1922.

Since independence, the Gorkhas have fought in every major campaign involving the Indian Army being awarded numerous battle and theatre honours. The regiments have won many gallantry awards like the Param Vir Chakra and the Maha Vir Chakra. The 8 Gorkha Rifles, has the unique distinction of producing one of the two Field Marshals of the Indian Army, Field Marshal Sam Manekshaw. He was the commanding officer of the 3rd battalion of the 8 Gorkha Rifles, and is still considered the most revered officer of the regiment.

5/5 Gorkha Rifles (Frontier Force) fought gallantly in Hyderabad Police in 1948. Naik Nar Bahadur Thapa of 5/5 Gorkha Rifles (Frontier Force) earned the first

Ashok Chakra Class I of independent India, in Hyderabad Police Action on 15 September 1948. The 4/5 Gorkha Rifles (Frontier Force) fought in the Battle of Sylhet, earning the distinction of being the first regiment of the Indian Army to be involved in a heliborne attack. Under the Indian Army, Gorkhas have served in Bangladesh, Sri Lanka, Siachen, and in the UN peacekeeping missions in Lebanon and Sierra Leone.

Major Dhan Singh Thapa of the 1/8 Gorkha Rifles won the Param Vir Chakra for his heroic actions during the 1962 Sino-Indian conflict. The 1st battalion of the 11 Gorkha Rifles was involved in Operation Vijay where Lt. (acting Captain) Manoj Kumar Pandey won the Param Vir Chakra for his gallant actions.

Current Strength

Currently there are 39 battalions serving in 7 Gorkha regiments in the Indian Army. Six regiments were transferred from the British Indian Army, one regiment was formed after independence. The following is a list of the Gorkha Regiments currently serving in the Indian Army:

- 1 Gorkha Rifles equipped with 5 battalions, previously 1st King George V's Own Gurkha Rifles (The Malaun Regiment);
- 3 Gorkha Rifles equipped with 5 battalions, previously 3rd Queen Alexandra's Own Gurkha Rifles.
- 4 Gorkha Rifles equipped with 5 battalions, previously 4th Prince of Wales's Own Gurkha Rifles
- 5 Gorkha Rifles (Frontier Force) equipped with 6 battalions, previously 5th Royal Gurkha Rifles (Frontier Force).
- 8 Gorkha Rifles equipped with 6 battalions, aka The Shiny Eight

- 9 Gorkha Rifles equipped with 6 battalions
- 11 Gorkha Rifles equipped with 6 battalions (Raised after the independence of India)

The individual Gorkha rifle regiments of India are collectively known for regimental purposes as the 'Gorkha Brigade' between themselves and are not to be confused with the Brigade of Gurkhas of the British Army.

In Popular Culture

A platoon of the 1/11 Gorkha Rifles, led by Lt. Manoj Kumar Pandey, has been depicted in the Bollywood movie LOC Kargil. Rais and Limbus who are collectively called as Kirnatis are also associated with the Mythological warrior Arjuna. Arjuna fought a duel with a Kiranti warrior who defeated him in the duel. The Kirantis in turn associate themselves with lord Shiva.

1 Gorkha Rifles

The 1 Gorkha Rifles is a Gorkha infantry regiment of the Indian Army. It was originally formed as part of the British Indian Army in 1815, later adopting the title of the 1st King George Vfs Own Gurkha Rifles (The Malaun Regiment), however, in 1947, following India's independence in 1947, it was transferred to the Indian Army and in 1950 when India became a Republic, it was redesignated as the 1 Gorkha Rifles (The Malaun Regiment). The regiment has a long tradition and has participated in many conflicts, including many of the colonial conflicts prior to Independence, as well as the First and Second World Wars. Since 1947 the regiment has also participated in a number of campaigns against Pakistan in 1965 and 1971 as well as undertaking peacekeeping duties as part of the United Nations.

History

Formation

The Gurkha War was fought between the Gorkha kings of Nepal and the British East India Company as a result of border tensions and ambitious expansionism especially into Kumaon, Garwhal and Kangra hills. Although the British East India Company's army defeated the Gorkha army led by General Amar Singh Thapa, they were nevertheless impressed by the skill and courage the Gorkhas had shown during the siege of Malaun fort in Bilaspur. As a result, during the post war settlement a clause was inserted into the Treaty of Segauli enabling the British to recruit Gorkhas. On 24 April 1815 at Subathu, the East India Company formed a regiment with the survivors of Thapa's army calling it the First Nusseree Battalion. This formation of this unit marks the beginning the of history of the first Gorkha regiment.

Early campaigns

The Regiment soon saw its first battle when, in 1826, it took part in the Jat War where it helped in the conquest of Bharatpur, gaining it as a Battle Honour, the first Battle Honour awarded to the Gurkha units. In 1846 the First Anglo-Sikh War began and the Regiment was heavily involved in the conflict. It was awarded two Battle honours for its involvement in the war; at the Battle of Aliwal which saw the Sikh forces, who had invaded British India.

The Regiment experienced numerous names changes during the 1800s; one name change in 1850 saw it gain a new numerical designation to become the 66th Goorkha Regiment of Bengal Native Infantry after the original 66th had mutinied. The Regiment saw service during the Indian Mutiny which began in 1857. The following year Lieutenant John Adam Tytler became the first Gurkha officer to be awarded the Victoria Cross (VC), receiving it for his actions against rebels at Choorpoorah.

In 1861 the Regiment gained its present numerical designation when it became the 1st Goorkha Regiment. In 1875 the Regiment was sent abroad for the first time, when it took parkin the effort to quell a rebellion in Malaya during the Perak War. During the conflict Captain George Nicolas Channer was awarded the Victoria Cross for his valiant actions against the Malayans. The Regiment took part in the Second Afghan War in 1878 where they were part of the 2nd Infantry Brigade and won the Theatre Honour "Afghanistan 1878-80".

In 1886 the Regiment became the 1st Goorkha Light Infantry and a 2nd Battalion was raised in February. In 1891 the Regiment was designated a Rifle regiment when it became the 1st Gurkha (Rifle) Regiment and in consequence of this the Regiment's Colours were laid up. The Regiment then took part in operations in Burma and the North-West Frontier campaigns in the 1890s; at Waziristan in 1894 and the Tirah campaign in 1897.

In 1901 the Regiment's title was shortened when it became the 1st Gurkha Rifles and in 1903 its title was changed once more, this time to the 1st Gurkha Rifles (The Malaun Regiment). This title had been adopted to commemorate due to the significance of Malaun to the Regiment; it was where the British had decisively beaten the Gurkhas in 1815 during the Anglo-Gurka War and subsequently recruited them into the Nusseree battalions. The Regiment was located near Dharamsala when the Kangra earthquake struck on 4 April 1905, killing 370,000 people. The 1st Gurkhas themselves suffered over 60 fatalities.

In 1906 its title was changed to the 1st Prince of Wales's Own Gurkha Rifles (The Malaun Regiment) in honour of HRH George, Prince of Wales (later King George V) who also became Colonel-in-Chief of the Regiment that year. In 1910 King George V ascended to the throne and in consequence the title of the regiment was changed to the 1st King George's Own Gurkha Rifles (The Malaun

Regiment), thus maintaining the Regiment's links with King George.

First World War

In August 1914 the First World War began. In December, the 1st Battalion was deployed to the Western Front in France as part of the Sirhind Indian Infantry Brigade, attached to 3rd (Lahore) Division. The 1st Battalion's first taste of trench warfare came when they were involved in the defence of Givenchy shortly after. After braving a winter in the trenches, on 10 March 1915 the 1st Battalion took part in the Battle of Neuve Chapelle which lasted until 13 March. In April the Battalion took part in the Second Battle of Ypres, fighting in the subsidiary Battle of St. Julien which began on 24 April and concluded on 4 May. Later that month the Battalion took part in the Battle of Festubert and in September the Battle of Loos began, the last major engagement on the Western Front that the 1st Battalion took part in, before being withdrawn from the Western Front.

The Western Front was a completely different location to what the Regiment had been used to in the sub-continent and they, as indeed did the other Indian Army troops, suffered badly during the winter months. As a result in December 1915 it was decided that the infantry units of the Indian Corps would be withdrawn from France and sent to other theatres. As a result the 1st Battalion, along with the rest of the 3rd Division, was sent to Mesopotamia to take part in the campaign against the Ottomans which had begun in 1914. The sirhind Brigade was given a numerical designation, the 8th Brigade. In 1916 the 1st Gurkhas took part in a number of attempts, including the attack on Dujaila Redoubt in March, to relieve Kut-al-Amara, which had been besieged by the Ottomans since 7 December 1915. Those attempts, however, failed and Kut remained under siege until it surrendered to the Ottomans on 29 April 1916.

Following this the Regiment took part in the Allied offensive against the Ottomans later that year; this included the effort to recapture Kut, begun in December, which was recaptured in February 1917 and the capital Baghdad which was taken the following month. The 1st Battalion was later moved to Palestine in early 1918. It was involved in the effective Allied offensive against the Ottomans in September, the Battle of Megiddo, and also saw action at the Sharon.

Elsewhere, the 2nd Battalion saw service in the North-West Frontier of India, gaining the Battle Honour "North-West Frontier 1915-17" in the process. In 1917 a 3rd Battalion was raised for home service in India.

During the period that they had served on the Western Front in France the men of the 1st Gurkhas had found the conditions quite different to those that they were used to, however, they acquitted themselves commendably, performing with distinction in the many battles they took part in, proving the capability of the Gurkhas once more. The war formally ended on 11 November 1918 with the signing of the Armistice. The Regiment won 11 Battle Honours and 4 Theatre Honours during the war.

Inter war years

In 1919 the 1st and 2nd Battalions saw service during the brief Third Afghan War for which they gained the Theatre Honour "Afghanistan 1919". In 1921 the 3rd Battalion was disbanded. After this the Regiment participated in a number of campaigns on the North-West Frontier, serving mainly in Waziristan.

In 1937 the Regiment's name was altered slightly when it became the 1st King George V's Own Gurkha Rifles (The Malaun Regiment); the only change being the addition of a V.

Second World War

In September 1939 the Second World War commenced

between the UK and its allies against Germany. In December 1941 the Japanese entered the war when it launched a surprise attack on Pearl Harbor and launched a number of swift invasions of British and other countries territories. During the course of the war the Regiment raised a further three battalions, the 3rd in 1940, the 4th in 1941 and the 5th in 1942; the Regiment saw much service in the war but most notably in Malaya and Burma.

The Regiment saw ferocious fighting during the Japanese invasion of Malaya; the 2nd Battalion, part of the 28th Brigade saw heavy fighting at Jitra where it was forced to hastily retreat after taking part in the initial resistance on the Asun and being isolated and confronted by overwhelming Japanese forces which included tanks. The 1st Battalion saw action at Kampar where they were out-numbered and sustained heavy casualties during an engagement at the Slim River Bridge on the 7 January. The Allies had withdrawn from Malaya, to Singapore, by January 1942. The Japanese subsequently launched an invasion of Singapore and bitter fighting ensued; Singapore, which had once been perceived as impregnable, fell on the 15 February 1942 with 130,000 British, Australian and Empire troops, including men of the 2nd Battalion, taken prisoner by the Japanese.

In Burma, a similar situation occurred, the Allies having to—having come under intense attacks from the Japanese who had begun their offensive in December—commence a retreat to India from February 1942 which was completed in May. Later, the battalions of the Regiment saw heavy fighting again in 1944 in the Arakan and during the Japanese offensive against north-east India where two important battles, Kohima and Imphal, took place from March to June 1944. Imphal was besieged by the Japanese until the Allies achieved a decisive victory at Kohima in June and the Japanese fled back into Burma. The Regiment subsequently took part in the successful Allied offensive into Burma and on the 3 May 1945 the Burmese capital Rangoon was liberated by British forces.

There were still Japanese forces present in Burma but the fight against the Japanese was now ostensibly a mopping up operation.

The war concluded with the formal surrender of Japan on 2 September 1945 on the deck of the USS Missouri in Tokyo Bay; the Allies had prevailed after nearly six years of fighting. In French Indochina that same day the Viet Minh, led by Ho Chi Minh, declared their independence from France as the Democratic Republic of Vietnam. Shortly afterwards the British began to send units of the 20th Indian Infantry Division, which the 1st and 3rd Battalions were part of, to occupy the south of the country while the Nationalist Chinese occupied the north; the deployment was completed by October. The force was intended to disarm the Japanese forces and help in their repatriation back to Japan. The force, however, soon became embroiled in the fight against the Viet Minh and was soon helping in the restoration of French-control over the country. The British were, due to a lack of sufficient manpower, ironically forced to have the Japanese forces working alongside their own in Indochina in order to maintain peace and stability. The operations against the Viet Minh gradually became more intense and after substantial French reinforcements arrived the British and Indian forces departed by May 1946, and the First Indochina War would begin shortly afterwards.

From September 1945 the 7th Indian Infantry Division, which the 4th Battalion was part of, was deployed to Siam (now Thailand) as part of an occupation force sent there to disarm the large Japanese forces present. The Battalion subsequently moved to Malaya in 1946 and then onto India.

In 1946, the 2nd Battalion, having been captured in Malaya in 1942, was reconstituted from personnel taken from the 3rd Battalion, which subsequently was disbanded along with the 4th and 5th Battalions.

Post Independence

This section requires expansion.

In 1947 an agreement, known as the Tripartite Agreement between India, Nepal and the United Kingdom was negotiated in order to determine what would happen to the Gurkhas upon the formalisation of India's Independence. As a result of this agreement it was decided that of the pre-war Gurkha regiments, four would be transferred to the British Army, while six—one of which was the 1st Gurkhas—would become part of the newly-independent Indian Army.

Despite India achieving its independence, the Regiment retained its full designation until 1950 when it became the 1 Gorkha Rifles (The Malaun Regiment), also adopting the Indian spelling of Gurkha, following India's transition to a republic.

Over time the wartime battalions that had been disbanded in 1946 were re-raised, so that by 1965 the Regiment consisted of five battalions once more.

In 1961 Captain Gurbachan Singh Salaria received the posthumous Param Vir Chakra (PVC), India's highest military honour, for his actions in the Congo when the 3rd Battalion, of which he was part, was on United Nations service.

Battle honours

- Bharatpur, Aliwal, Sobraon, Afghanistan 1878-80, Tirah, Punjab Frontier;
- *First World War:* Givenchy 1914, Neuve Chapelle, Ypres 1915, St. Julien, Festubert 1915, Loos, France and Flanders 1914-15, Megiddo, Sharon, Palestine 1918, Tigris 1916, Kut al Amara 1917, Baghdad, Mesopotamia 1916 18;
- N.W. Frontier India 1915-17, Afghanistan 1919;
- *Second World War:* Jitra, Kampar, Malaya 1941-42,

Shenam Pass, Bishenpur, Ukhrul, Myinmu Bridgehead, Kyaukse 1945, Burma 1942-45;

- *Post Independence:* Kalidhar, Jammu and Kashmir 1965, Darsana, Jammu and Kashmir 1971, East Pakistan 1971.

Valour awards

- Victoria Cross

GORKHA RIFLES

The 3 Gorkha Rifles is an Indian Army infantry regiment. It was originally a Gurkha regiment of the British Indian Army formed in 1815. They were present at a number of actions and wars including the Siege of Delhi in 1857 to the First and Second World Wars. After the Partition of India in 1947 the regiment was one of the six Gorkha regiments transferred to the Indian Army as part of the Tripartite Agreement signed between India, Nepal and Britain at the time of Indian independence. Prior to independence, the regiment was known as the 3rd Queen Alexandra's Own Gurkha Rifles. In 1950 the regiment's title was changed to 3 Gorkha Rifles. Since 1947 the regiment has participated in a number of conflicts including the 1947 and 1971 wars against Pakistan.

Formation to 1885

The regiment was raised during the Gurkha War by Sir Robert Colquhoun on 24 April 1815 as the Kemaoon Battalion. It did not consist entirely of Gurkhas but of men from Kumaon and Garhwal. The regiment adopted the tartan of the Clan Colquhoun.

The regiment was primarily used to police the border with Nepal, doing so for many decades until the Indian Mutiny began in 1857. The battalion was actively involved in the efforts to quell it. During the Siege of Delhi—which lasted from March to September 1857—the regiment, part of Colonel Colin Campbell's Third Column, took part in the storming of Kashmiri Gate and gained the Battle Honour "Delhi 1857". The mutiny was quelled by July 1858.

The regiment, having been brought into the line of the Bengal Army, was briefly titled the 18th Bengal Native Infantry in 1861 before the regiment gained its present numeral designation when it became the 3rd Goorka (The Kumaon) Regiment. The regiment saw service in an expedition to Bhutan shortly after the name change.

In 1878 the Second Afghan War began and the regiment, as part of the 2nd Infantry Brigade of the Kandahar Field Force, took part in the march to seize Kandahar. The field force successfully captured the city on 8 January 1879, having experienced great hardship on the march there. The following year the Kandahar Force began the march towards the Afghan capital Kabul to join Major-General Roberts force in an attempt to consolidate their situation in the country. During the journey, near Ghaziri, the force were attacked by a large force of Afghan tribesmen at Ahmad Khel on 19 April 1880. The fighting that ensued was intense and the field force's situation was in the balance until the Afghan forces were successfully repulsed when the 3rd Goorkhas formed an infantry square.

1885-1914

The regiment took part in the Third Burmese War after it began in 1885 and operations concluded by the following year. In 1887 the 2nd Battalion was formed, consisting entirely of Garhwalis, but this was separated from the regiment in 1890 to form the 39th (The Garhwal) Regiment of Bengal Light Infantry. A new 2nd Battalion for the 3rd Goorkhas was raised that same year and in 1891 the Regiment was designated a rifle regiment, becoming the 3rd Gurkha (Rifle) Regiment.

The 3rd Gurkhas took part in numerous campaigns

in the volatile North-West Frontier, including the 1st Battalion's participation in the storming of the Dargai Heights on 20 October 1897 during the Tirah Campaign. The battalion was part of the Tirah Field Force intended to put down a large tribal revolt by the Afridi and Orakzais, orchestrated by Afghanistan. The 3rd Gurkhas took part in the advance into the Tirah Region, meeting resistance from tribal forces before moving on to help relieve Fort Lockheart and Fort Gulistan. After this was done the force marched on Dargai where they intended to take the heights above Dargai, controlled by tribal forces.

The heights had originally been taken by the Tirah force on 18 October but they were ordered to withdraw, coming under attack as they did so and allowing the tribal force to return to the heights and strengthen their positions. The operation to retake the heights began with an artillery bombardment at 10:00am on 20 October. The regiment took part in the initial assault, positioned at the forefront of the attack with the 2nd Gurkha Rifles and the 1st Dorsets. They advanced methodically, moving up the slopes until they charged towards the enemy but sustained heavy casualties and became pinned down. The battle raged on for hours until, after the tribal positions were subject to an artillery bombardment, a final charge was made by the 1st Gordons, followed by the Gurkhas and 3rd Sikhs. The tribal defenders wilted in the face of the charge and the heights were taken later that day.

In 1907 the title was changed to become the 3rd The Queen's Own Gurkha Rifles in honour of Alexandra of Denmark, queen consort of King Edward VII, and the following year the title became more specific when it became the 3rd Queen Alexandra's Own Gurkha Rifles.

First World War

In August 1914 the First World War began and the

regiment's battalions actively participated on the Western Front and in the Middle East.

In 1916, a clerical error gave the regiment a 4th Battalion when 4/3rd, instead of 3/4th, was written on the order for the raising of a battalion for the 4th Gurkha Rifles. The following year a 3rd Battalion for the 3rd Gurkhas was formed.

Western Front

The 2nd Battalion, as part of the Garwhal Brigade of the 7th (Meerut) Division, was sent to France a few months after the declaration of war in 1914.

The battalion's first large-scale action came at La Bassee that had commenced on 12 October as part of a period known as the "Race to the Sea". The battalion was involved in the defence of Festubert in November and Givenchy in December, during a bitter winter that the Gurkhas were no doubt unaccustomed to having spent the inter-war period on the sub-continent.

The battalion remained on the Western Front until late 1915. At the Battle of Neuve Chapelle (10-13 March) the Garwhal Brigade advanced successfully during the initial offensive and the 1st Battalion took part in fierce fighting during the battle. In May it was involved in the battles of Festubert and Aubers. In September the battalion took part in the Battle of Loos which saw the regiment awarded its first Victoria Cross. The VC action took place on 25 September when Rifleman Kulbir Thapa of the 2nd Battalion performed with distinction near the village of Fauqissart, becoming the first Gurkha recipient of the award.

The Battle of Loos was the battalion's last action on the Western Front and it left the 7th Division with the rest of the Garhwal Brigade for Egypt in December 1915 after the brigade became an independent unit.

Middle East

After its arrival in Egypt the 2nd Battalion saw active service against the Ottoman Empire and later took part in the Palestine campaign, the second largest campaign by force totals during the First World War. It fought in the Autumn Offensive, seeing their first action during the Battles of Gaza. It was involved in many other actions during the campaign, including the capture of Jerusalem in December. On 19 September 1918, just a few months before the conclusion of the war, the Megiddo Offensive, began and the battalion was involved in the capture of Sharon. For its part in the campaign the 3rd Gurkhas gained seven Battle Honours and the Theatre Honour "Palestine 1917-18" after such honours were granted to units in the 1920s.

On 10 April 1918 at El Kefr in Egypt, Karanbahadur Rana of the 2nd Battalion became the regiment's second VC recipient after distinguishuing himself in an encounter with Ottoman forces, and was the last VC recipient of the regiment.

Elsewhere the 1st Battalion, from 1917, took part in the Mesopotamian Campaign (now Iraq), gaining only a single Battle Honour in the process. It was achieved at the last battle of the campaign, at the Battle of Sharqat (28-30 October 1918).

1919-1939

The First World War concluded with the signing of the Armistice on 11 November 1918 but this gave the regiment no respite. It took part in the Third Afghan War in 1919 and spent much of their inter-war years in the North West Frontier and Burma. The post-war reductions saw the regiment reduced to its pre-war establishment. The 3rd Battalion was disbanded in 1920 and the mistakenly raised 4th Battalion followed in 1922.

Second World War

The regiment was actively involved in Second World War and, as had happened during the First World War, the regiment was expanded to meet its commitments. The 3rd Battalion was re-raised in 1940, followed by the 4th Battalion in 1941. During the conflict, the regiment fought in a number of theatres, including North Africa, Italy and Burma. During the North African campaign, the 2nd Battalion fought at Tobruk, where they were brought in as reinforcements at the height of the battle and suffered misfortune almost immediately, when they were partially overrun by the Germans, losing almost two hundred men as prisoners of war, although many of these managed to escape later.

Post Independence

India gained its independence in 1947 and the regiment was one of six Gurkha regiments (out of 10) to be allocated to the Indian Army as part of the Tripartite Agreement between Britain, India and Nepal. The regiment retained its title until 1950 when India was proclaimed a Republic and the regiment became the 3 Gorkha Rifles. It remains in existence and consists of five battalions.

The Regiment won the Battle Honour 'Pir Kanthi' in the Uri Sector in the war of 1948 and 'Shingo' in the Kargil Sector in war of 1971. 1/3 GR has the distinction of being the first battalion in the post-independence period to carry out amphibious operations during the 1971 Indo-Pak War. Colonel J.R. Chitnis, CO 1/3 GR, was honoured with the Ashoka Chakra posthumously—India's highest peacetime medal for valour—in Nagaland in 1956.

On 3 December 1997, a statue was unveiled in London in honour of the Gurkhas. A quote from Sir Ralph Turner, a former officer in the 3rd Gurkhas, was inscribed on the memorial: *"Bravest of the brave, most generous of the generous, never had country more faithful friends than you.*

4 GORKHA RIFLES

The 4 Gorkha Rifles is an infantry regiment of the Indian Army. It was originally raised in 1857 as part of the British Indian Army, but after India's independence in 1947 it was one of six Gurkha regiments transferred to the Indian Army. The regiment was formerly known as the 4th Prince of Wales's Own Gurkha Rifles, but after it was transferred to the Indian Army its name was changed upon India becoming a republic. Since its establishment over 150 years ago, the regiment has fought in many conflicts and earned many battle honours, including the Second Afghan War, the Boxer Rebellion, the First World War, the Second World War and most of the wars and Counter Insurgency Operations India has fought since independence.

Early History

In 1857, it was decided to augment the existing Gurkha regiments by raising another. Initially, this was known as the Extra Goorkha Regiment, before being numbered as the 19th Regiment of Bengal Native Infantry. In 1861 it was finally designated as the 4th Goorkha Regiment.

The regiment's first major action came during the Second Afghan War, although in this time it also served on the North-West Frontier and during the Boxer Rebellion in 1900.

The regiment's first Victoria Cross came during operations in Somalia during the Third Somaliland Campaign in 1903, when then Captain William George Walker risked his life in an attempt to save the life of another officer who had been wounded during earlier fighting. Walker's VC was, however, earning serving in the Somali Camel Corps, not the 4th Gorkhas.

First World War

During the First World War, the 1st Battalion served in

France, participating in the battles of Givenchy, Neuve Chapelle and Ypres, while the 2nd Battalion saw service in Mesopotamia. A 3rd Battalion was authorised to be raised, but due to a clerical error, the 4th Battalion, 3rd Gurkha Rifles was raised instead of the 3rd Battalion, 4th Gurkha Rifles.

In 1924, the regiment became the 4th Prince of Wales's Own Gurkha Rifles, with the Prince of Wales becoming Colonel-in-Chief.

Second World War

The regiment saw service in most theatres during the Second World War, including the Middle East, North Africa, Italy, and the Far East.

The 1st Battalion served throughout the Burma Campaign. During the early part of the campaign the battalion fought in the Battle of Sittang Bridge. It was commanded at this engagement and during the subsequent retreat into India by Lieutenant Colonel "Joe" Lentaigne, who later succeeded Major General Orde Wingate in charge of the Chindits. Later, during the Battle of Imphal, the battalion suffered nearly 100% casualties (and an even higher percentage of losses among officers). The 2nd Battalion saw service in Iraq and Syria. It was overrun by two Bersaglieri battalions of the Italian Trento Division storming the fortress of Mersa Matruh on 29 June 1942, but was rebuilt and subsequently fought in the Italian Campaign.

The 3rd Battalion was finally raised in 1940. It saw service with the Chindits in Burma. The 4th Battalion was raised in 1941. It also fought in Burma, distinguishing itself by storming Mandalay Hill in 1945.

A prominent figure who was pa.t of the 4th Gurkha Rifles during the thirties and the Second World War was the author John Masters, who participated in operations on the North West Frontier, in Iraq, the Second

Chindit Operation, the capture of Mandalay and at one point commanded the 3rd Battalion of the regiment. His autobiographical books "Bugles and a Tiger" and "The Road past Mandalay" portray life in the Indian Army and the 4th Gurkha Rifles during this period.

Post 1947

Following India's independence in 1947, the 4th Gurkhas was one of the Gorkha regiments to be allocated to the Indian Army. In 1950, when India became a republic, the regiment's name was changed to the 4th Gorkha Rifles as it was decided to adopt the Indian spelling.

The centre at Bakloh was abandoned as the Gorkha regimental training centres were merged. As a result, the 4th's training centre was merged with that of the 1st Gorkha Rifles and located at Subathu.

The 4th Gorkhas have distinguished themselves in the three Indo-Pakistan Wars of 1947, 1965 and 1971 being awarded battle and theatre honours for all three conflicts. The third battalion fought a fine action at Bilafond La, at heights of nearly 20,000 feet (6,100 m) in 1987.

The 1st Battalion (JETHI) was awarded the COAS Unit Citation in 2002, for its performance in counter terrorism operations in Kupwara district, Kashmir. The Battalion was commended for neutralizing 94 Foreign Terrorists, in a number of operations in Tangdhar, Panzgam and Lolab. The Battalion suffered two fatal casualties, Capt Anirban Bandhyopadhyay and Nb Sub Deb Bahadur Thapa. They were posthumously awarded the Sena Medal and the Kirti Chakra respectively.

The Regiment is unique in the Indian Army, as the battalions do not celebrate individual Raising Days. Regimental Day (called Neuve Chapelle-Baghdad Day) is celebrated on 11 March by the entire Regiment, commemorating the 1st Battalion's entry in the Battle of Neuve Chapelle in France and the 2nd Battalion's entry into Baghdad on that day (albeit in different years), during the First World War.

The Regiment derives most of its drills and standards from the British 'Greenjackets', and marches 'quickstep' at 180 paces a minute. The Pipeband of the First Battalion is one of the finest in the Indian Army. The uniform and insignia are Spartan, and a healthy disdain for pomp or being 'Red' is central to the Regiment's identity and professional approach. The 4th Gorkhas are also the only Regiment in the Indian Army who wear the Lanyard (a plain Black) over the Jersey. This is again taken from the British Rifles Regiment, where only those exercising command over men wear a lanyard for the whistle. The right hand occupied by the sword, the left is free to draw the whistle - easier done from the right pocket. Many erroneously believe that lanyard is worn on the Right shoulder only by the erstwhile 'Royal' regiments, and the 4th Gurkhas do so because they were the 'Prince of Wales' Own'. This is wrong. A regiment's 'Royal' status is marked by the colour of the lanyard (Red) and the prefix 'Royal' only. Many Indian Army units have dropped their pre-independence prefix of 'Royal', but still wear the Red Lanyard.

The Regiment celebrated its Sesquicentenary in 2007

Battle Honours

Pre First World War

- Ali Masjid
- Kabul 1879
- Kandahar 1880
- Afghanistan 1878-80
- Chitral
- Waziristan 1895
- Tirah

- Punjab Frontier
- China 1900.

First World War

- Givenchy 1914
- Neuve Chapelle
- Yprcs 1915
- St. Julien
- Aubers
- Festubert 1915
- France and Flanders 1914-15
- Egypt 1916
- Tigris 1916
- Kutal Amara 1917
- Baghdad
- Mesopotamia 1916-18
- Gallipoli 1915
- N.W. Frontier India 1917
- Baluchistan 1918.

Inter War Period

- Afghanistan 1919

Second World War

- Iraq 1941
- Syria 1941
- The Cauldron
- North Africa 1940-43
- Trestina
- Monte Cedrone
- Italy 1943-45

- Pegu 1942
- Chindits 1944
- Bishenpur
- Shwebo
- Mandalay
- Burma 1942-45

Post Independence

- Punch
- Gurais
- Jammu and Kashmir 1947-48
- Punjab 1965
- Jammu and Kashmir 1971 COAS Unit Citation, 2002.

Gallantry Awards

Pre-independence

1 Victoria Cross 1 Commander of the British Empire 10 Distinguished Service Order - 1 Order of the British Empire - 1 Bar to DSO - 24 Military Cross - 1 Bar to MC - 1 Member of the British Empire - 1 French Legion of Honour - 96 Mention in Despatches - 9 Order of British India - 15 Indian Order of Merit - 6 IDM - 42 Indian Distinguished Service Medal - 1 Croix De Guerre - 11 Medialle Militaire - 1 Bronze Medal for Military Valour - 1 Medal of Saint George - 2 Star of Nepal

Post-independence

3 Param Vishishth Seva Medal - 1 Maha Vir Chakra - 1 Kirti Chakra - 3 Ati Vishishtha Seva Medal - 5 Vir Chakra - 2 Shaurya Chakra - 1 Yudh Seva Medal - 24 Sena Medals - 6 Vishishtha Seva Medals - 9 Mention in Dispatches - 40 Commendation cards.

5 GORKHA RIFLES

The 5 Gorkha Rifles (Frontier Force) is an infantry regiment of the Indian Army comprising Gurkha soldiers of Nepal ese origin. It was formed in 1858 as part of the British Indian Army and served in the First World War and Second World War. The regiment was one of the Gorkha regiments that was transferred to the Indian Army following independence in 1947. The regiment was formerly known as the 5th Royal Gurkha Rifles (Frontier Force). Since 1947, the regiment has served in a number of conflicts, including the Indo-Pakistani War of 1965 and the Indo-Pakistani War of 1971. It has also participated in peacekeeping operations in Sri Lanka.

History

19th Century

The regiment was raised in 1858 as the 25th Punjab Infantry. The soldiers of the regiment originated from the Kingdom of Nepal and in 1861 it was renamed the 5th Gurkha Regiment. The regiment's first major action was during the Second Afahan War, where they were awarded their first battle honour at Peiwar Kotal and Captain John Cook was awarded the Victoria Cross. In 1891 the regiment was afforded the prestigious title of a Rifle regiment and became 5th Gurkha (Rifle) Regiment which was shortened to 5th Gurkha Rifles in 1901.

The regiment spent most of its time up to the end of the 19th century based in the Punjab as part of the Punjab Frontier Force, more famously known as PFF or Piffers. This was reflected when in 1903, when the regiment was renamed the 5th Gurkha Rifles (Frontier Force).

First World War

During the First World War, the regiment primarily saw service in the Middle East—the 1st Battalion saw extensive service at Gallipoli in 1915 (where 7 officers and 129 men were killed in the first few hours after the battalion landed). During the withdrawal, the last troops to leave was a company of the 5th Gurkhas.

The 2nd Battalion saw service in Mesopotamia, initially with the 2nd (Rawalpindi) Division and from April 1916 with the 15th Division. The 1st Battalion joined them in March 1917 from the 1st (Peshawar) Division and both battalions fought together at the Action of Khan Baghdad!. A 3rd Battalion was raised for service on the North-West Frontier, before being disbanded in 1921.

Inter-War Period

In 1921, the regiment was given the title the 5th Royal Gurkha Rifles, in recognition of its service during the war. During the inter-war period, the regiment received three further battle honours, for the Third Afghan War in 1919, and two for service on the North West Frontier. The regiment together with the 13th Duke of Connaught's Own Lancers were the only units awarded such honours.

Second World War

During the Second World War, the 1st Battalion 5th Gurkhas as part of the 8th Indian Infantry Division's 17th Indian Infantry Brigade served in the Middle East campaign and the Italian Campaign. Rifleman Thaman Gurung of the 1st Battalion won the Victoria Cross while serving in Italy.

The 2nd Battalion served in the Far East in the Burma Campaign as part of the 17th Indian Infantry Division and was involved in the retreat of the British Indian Army from Burma, they were one of four battalions chosen to fight as the rearguard at the Sittang River, which formed the border with India. When the bridge over the river was blown up preventing the Japanese forces from entering India, many of the regiment were left on the wrong side. The regiment was involved in the re-entry into Burma in 1943 where three members of the regiment were awarded the Victoria Cross. After the war, the 2nd Battalion was re-issued with new uniforms, equipment and transport and posted to Tokyo in Japan as part of the British Commonwealth Occupation Forced

The 4th Battalion was raised in 1941 and also served in the Burma Campaign as part of the 7th Indian Infantry Division, fighting in five epic battles at North Arakan, Buthidaung (Battle of the Admin Box), Kohima, Pokkoku (Irrawaddy) and Sittang. The Battalion had the unique distinction of getting four Battle Honours for the five battles fought. Major I M Brown of the 4th Battalion was one of the few soldiers of the Second World War that was awarded the Military Cross three times.

Post Independence

On Independence, the 5th Royal Gurkha Rifles was one of the six Gurkha regiments that remained part of the new Indian Army, they were renamed the 5th Gorkha Rifles (Frontier Force) in 1950. The Regiment now has a total of six Battalions and has, participated in virtually every major action the Indian Army has undertaken in its four wars with Pakistan, including the first airborne operations undertaken by the army during the 1971 war. The Regiment has participated in the following actions:

- Indo-Pak War of 1947-48
- Indo-Pakistani War of 1965
- Battle of Topa (Jammu and Kashmir)
- Battle of Atgram (East Pakistan) 1971
- Battle of Sylhet (East Pakistan) 1971
- Battle of Gazipur (East Pakistan - Banglasdesh) 1971

The 4th Battalion was also a part of the Indian Peace Keeping Force which served in Sri Lanka and fought with LTTE. This is where Col Bawa was injured and later died, with many of his officers and soldiers.

Lineage

1858-1861 — 25th Punjab Infantry

1861-1891 — 5th Gurkha Regiment

1891-1901 — 5th Gurkha (Rifle) Regiment

1901-1903 — 5th Gurkha Rifles

1903-1950 — 5th Gurkha Rifles (Frontier Force)

1950-present — 5th Gorkha Rifles (Frontier Force).

Battle Honours

- *19th Century:* Peiwar Kotal, Charasiah, Kabul 1879, Kandahar 1880, Afghanistan 1878-80, Punjab Frontier;
- *First World War:* Suez Canal, Egypt 1915-16, Khan Baghdadi, Mesopotamia 1916-18, Helles, Krithia, Suvla, Sari Bair, Gallipoli 1915, North West Frontier 1917;
- *Inter War Years:* Afghanistan 1919, North West Frontier 1930, North West Frontier 1936-39;
- *Second World War:* The Sangro, Caldari, Cassino II, San Angelo in Teodice, Rocca d'Arce, Ripa Ridge, Femmina Morta, Monte San Bartolo, The Senio, Italy 1943-45, Sittang 1942, Yenangyaung 1942, Buthidaung, Stockades, North Arakan, Chindits 1944, Mogaung, Imphal, Sakawng, Shenam Pass, Bishenpur, The Irrawaddy 1942-45, Sittang 1945, Burma 1942-45;
- *Post Independence:* Zoji La, Kargil, Jammu and Kashmir 1947-48, Charwa, Punjab 1965, Sylhet, East Pakistan 1971, Jammu and Kashmir 1971, Shehjra, Punjabi 971.

Victoria Cross Recipients

There were seven Victoria Crosses awarded to British

officers and Gurkhas serving with the regiment prior to 1947:

- Captain John Cook — Afghanistan, 2 December 1878
- Lieutenant Guy Boisragon — Hunza, 2 December 1891
- Lieutenant John Manners-Smith — Hunza, 20 December 1891
- Havildar Gaje Ghale — Burma, 27 May 1943
- Naik Agansing Rai — Burma, 26 June 1944
- Jemadar Netra bahadur Thapa — Burma, 26 June 1944
- Riflemann Thaman Gurung — Italy, 10 November 1944

Maha Vir Chakra Receipients

- Lieutenant Colonel Anant Singh Pathania, MC
- L/Havildar Ram Prasad Gurung
- Major General H K Sibal
- Brigadier Z C Bakshi
- Brigadier M L Whig
- Lieutenant Colonel (Later Brigadier) Arun Bhimrao Harolikar
- Rifleman (Later Havildar) Dil Bahadur Chettri
- Lieutenant Colonel Inder Bal Singh Bawa {Posthumous}

8 GORKHA RIFLES

The 8 Gorkha Rifles is a Gorkha regiment of the Indian Army. It was raised in 1824 as part of the British East India Company and later transferred to the British Indian Army after the Indian Rebellion of 1857. The regiment served in the World War I and World War II, before being one of the Gurkha regiments transferred to the Indian Army after independence in 1947. Since then it has served in a number of conflicts including the Sino-Indian War of 1962 and the Indo-Pakistan wars of 1965 and 1971. Today the 8th Gorkha Rifles is one of the most celebrated regiments of the Indian Army, having received numerous citations for bravery in the field of battle, and even producing one of the two field marshals, Field Marshal Sam Manekshaw, of the Indian Army.

History

Formation and Early Campaigns

The "Shiny Eight", as the regiment is popularly known in the Gorkha fraternity of the Indian Army, can trace its history back to the 16th Sylhet Local Battalion, which was raised in 1824 as part of the British East India Company and since then the identity of the Regiment has undergone a number of transitions before reaching its present designation as the 8 Gorkha Rifles, which it achieved in 1907.

Military assignments commenced as soon after the raising of the Regiment when the first battalion formed the spearhead for operations in the First Anglo-Burmese War of 1824-25. The services of the Regiment were to be requisitioned again when the British went to war with Bhutan in 1864. Two battalion columns of the Regiment sallied forth, shoulder to shoulder to crush the Bhutanese revolts and the stronghold of Devnageri. The first Victoria Cross (VC), awarded to Richard Ridgeway, came to the Regiment in October 1879 in its first ever operational mission when its units were summoned to deal with Nagaland Rebels. This was the first time that a regular army unit was ever been employed in the Naga hills.

The Regiment's second Victoria Cross was awarded to Charles Grant, for his actions on the during the

Manipur Expedition on the North-East Frontier on 27 March 1891 whilst attached to the 2nd Battalion. Following the disaster at Manipur, Grant volunteered to attempt the relief of the British who were being held captive with a force of 80 Gurkhas. Inspiring his men with his example of personal daring and resource, the lieutenant captured Thobal, near Manipur, from a force of 800 Manipuris on 30 March 1891. For the next ten days Grant and his small force held Thobal, before on 9 April 1891, having run out of food and having almost no ammunition left, they were forced to abandon the position. In his report following the incident, Lieutenant Grant recommended every member of his party be awarded the Indian Order of Merit, which was at that time the highest award a native member of the British Indian Army could be awarded. This recommendation was later accepted and all of Grant's men were also rewarded with six months pay and allowances.

The Younghusband Expedition of 1904 was another operation that brought a VC to the Regiment, awarded to John Duncan Grant—no relation to Charles Grant—for his actions during the British expedition to Tibet. Braving the high altitude climes of Tibet, the expeditionary force successfully stormed the Tibetan fortress of Gyantse at 18,000 feet.

World War I

World War I (1914-18) testified to the enigmatic valour and heroism of the Regiment during the course of combat service in Italy, France, Mesopotamia (present-day Iraq) and Egypt. During the fighting in France, the 2nd/8th distinguished itself by fighting virtually to the last man during the Battle of Loos on 25 September 1915, hurling themselves time after time against the weight of German defences. Having mustered almost eight hundred men to begin with, by the end of the day they had a frontage of just one officer and forty-nine men.

The Regiment won 14 battle honours during this period:

- La Bassee, Festubert, Givenchy, Neauve Chapelle, Aubers, France and Flanders 1914-15; Egypt, Megiddo, Sharon, Palestine, Tigris, Kut-at-Amara, Baghdad, Mesopotamia 1916-18.

Following the war, it also participated in the Third Afghan War, earning the Afghanistan 1919 battle honour.

Inter War Years

During the years between the two World Wars, the 8th Goorkhas were based in India, where they undertook various garrison duties, in between service on the North West Ftontier. It was whilst the 2/8th was based at Quetta in the mid 1930s that a member of the Regiment would display outstanding courage, this time not during war but during peace. In 1935 a series of powerful earthquakes rocked north-west India and thousands of people were killed. The men of the 2/8th worked tirelessly in their efforts to help free many of the civilians that were caught beneath the ruins. Nandlal Thapa received the Empire Gallantry Medal for repeatedly risking his life entering buildings that were in danger of collapsing amidst the aftershocks in order to rescue injured survivors. At the time the Empire Gallantry Medal was the highest award for gallantry for actions performed not in the face of the enemy, although later when the George Cross came into being in 1940, Nandlal Thapa received the George Cross to replace his Empire Gallantry Medal.

World War II

The Regiment's battalions also saw active overseas actions in Iraq, Egypt, Libya, Tobruk, El Alamein and Burma during World War II where the Regiment earned its fourth VC and twenty-two battle honours. Lachhiman Gurung was awarded the VC during the Burmese Campaign. In

January 1943 the 2nd Battalion was attached to the 3rd Indian Motor Brigade which had just returned from the Western Desert after having been almost destroyd at the Battle of Gazala. At the end of the month the brigade was renamed as the 43rd Indian Infantry Brigade (Lorried). The brigade and its Gurkha battalions were sent to Italy in mid 1944 as an Independent brigade.

The Regiment's World War II Battle Honours include:

- Iraq 1941, North Africa 1940-43, Gothic Line, Coriano, Sant' Angelo, Gaiana Crossing, Point 551, Italy 1942-44; Tamu Road, Bishenpur, Kanglatongbi, Mandalay, Myinmu Bridgehead, Singhu, Shan-datgyi, Sittang, Imphal, Burma 1942-15.

Post Independence

The 8th Gurkha Rifles, along with the 1st, 3rd, 4th, 5th, and 9th Gurkha Rifles, was transferred to India on independence in 1947. The regiment became one of the Gorkha regiments (India) when the spelling was changed for all of the transferred regiments.

Kashmir Operations

Soon after partition, the 2/8 Gorkha Rifles saw action in the Leh operations of 1948. The battalion made a forced march over inhospitable terrain and reached Leh. Major Hari Chand and his company were involved in a series of raids that demoralized the Pakistani forces, this included destruction of the Pakistani mountain guns at the village of Basgo which had been brought in to consolidate the raiders hold over Leh. In this action, Major Hari Chand and four other ranks were awarded the Maha Vir Chakra (MVC) and Vir Chakra (VRC) respectively.

Sino-Indian War of 1962

One Param Vir Chakra was awarded to Major Dhan Singh

Thapa, of the 1/8 Gorkha Rifles, during the Sino Indian War. To date this is the only recipient of the Param Vir Chakra for the Regiment.

Later Period

The Regiment was also involved in the 1965 and 1971 Indo-Pakistan conflicts during which members of the regiment were awarded 4 Maha Vir Chakras. The Regiment was also actively involved in the operations in Sri Lanka where again members of the regiment were awarded fo gallantry winning one Maha Vir Chakra and four Vir Chakras.

In 1979 when the 1/8 became a Mechanised Infantry Regiment, a further battalion was raised on July 1, 1979 and named the 7/8 Gorkha Rifles.

Notable Officers

The Regiment produced one Chief of Indian Army, Field Marshal SHFJ Manekshaw, MC and is incidentally the most celebrated personality of the Regiment. His contribution in the 1971 Indo-Pak War is a legend in the military history of India's Armed Forces. In addition to Sam the Regiment has produced a number of army commanders in independent India, notably amongst them is Lt Gen RK Nanavatty.

9 GORKHA RIFLES

The 9 Gorkha Rifles is a Gorkha regiment of the Indian Army. The regiment was one of the Gurkha regiments transferred to the Indian Army after independence as part of the tripartite agreement. This Gorkha regiment dominantly recruits soldiers from Bahun, Chhetri (Kshatriya) and Thakuri clans. Domiciled Indian Gorkhas are also taken, who form about 20 percent of the total strength of the regiment.

History

The history of the 9 Gorkha Rifles dates back to 1817, when it was raised at Infantry Levy at Fatehgarh as Fatehgarh Levy. In 1823, it became 63rd Regiment a regular unit as part of the Bengal Native Infantry. After the reorganisations post-1857, the designation was changed to 9th Bengal Native Infantry with one of its companies formed by Gorkhas and other hillmen. By then the Regiment had fought at Bhartpur and in the difficult Battle of Sobraon in the First Anglo-Sikh War.

By 1893, the regiment became a wholly Gorkha unit of Khas origin, *i.e.*, those who were more closely linked to Hindu ways as compared to the Buddhist ways. In 1903, the Regiment was designated 9th Gurkha Rifles.

9 GR fought in the Great War in Europe and in the inter war years took part in the operations in the North-West Frontier. In World War II, it fought in Italy and North Africa. The 3/9 GR and 4/9 GR formed part of the Chindit operations in Burma, and earned a reputation in the long range penetration operations.

Post Independence

India gained its independence in 1947 and 9 Gorkha Rifles was one of six Gurkha regiments (out of 10) to be allocated to the Indian Army as part of the Tripartite Agreement between Britain, India and Nepal. Since 1947 the regiment has fought in the 1962 Indo-China War, the 1/9 GR fought under the most demanding conditions on the Namka Chu in (Arunachal Pradesh). The Regiment was also involved in the 1965 and 1971 wars with Pakistan.

Titles of the Regiment and its Predecessor

(1817-1819) Fatagarh Levy

(1819-1824) Mianpuri Levy

(1824-1861) 63rd Regiment of Bengal Native Infantry

(1861-1885) 9th Regiment of Bengal Native Infantry

(1885-1894) 9th Regiment of Bengal Infantry

(1894-1901) 9th (Gurkha Rifle) Bengal Infantry

(1903-1947) 9th Gurkha Rifles

(1950-present) 9 Gorkha Rifles

Battle honours

- Pre Independence

Bharatpur, Sabraon, Afghanistan (1879-80), Punjab Frontier, La Bassee, Festubert, Armentiers, Givenchy, Neuve Chapelle, Aubers, Laos, France and Flanders, Tigris, Kut-al-Amara, Mesopotamia, Djebel-el-Maida, Djebel Garci, Ragoubet Scuissi, Chindit, Tavoleto, Hangman's Hill, San Marino, Baghdad and Cassino.

Victoria Cross Recipients

- Major later Lt. Colonel George Campbell Wheeler, 2nd Battalion, 23 February 1917, River Tigris, Mesopotamia.
- Temp Major Frank Gerald Blaker, Highland Light Infantry, attached to 3rd Battalion, 9 July 1944, Taunggyi, Burma (now Myanmar).
- Rifleman Sher Bahadur Thapa, 1st Battalion, 18 September 1944, San Marino, Italy.

11 GORKHA RIFLES

The 11 Gorkha Rifles is a Gorkha regiment of the Indian Army that was re-raised after independence. The regiment consists of primarily the Rais and Limbus of eastern Nepal. The Rais and Limbus are supposed to be fierce tribal warriors of Nepal and are considered to be most sturdy and tough they also claim to have a relationship with the mythological warrior Kirant who fought and defeated legendary warrior Arjuna in Mahabharata. Though it is considered to be the youngest of the Gorkha Regiments it has a lineage which is as old as the history of the 7th Gurkhas and 10th Gurkhas. First Regiment

The 11th Gurkhas was raised as an ad hoc unit in 1918 with troops and officers being drawn from the various Gurkha Regiments. This regiment saw service in both Palestine and Mesopotamia at the end of the First World War, as well as during the Third Afghan War in 1919, before being disbanded in 1922 and the troops being reverted to their original units. There were no separate insignias authorized for this regiment and the personnel wore the badges of distinction of their parent units, though there have been instances where unofficial badges were made and worn by some personnel.

Second Regiment

Following India's independence in 1947, the Gurkha regiments of the British Indian Army were divided between the new Indian Army and the British Army. A referendum was held among the soldiers of the four regiments (2nd, 6th, 7th and 10th Gurkhas) that would transfer to the British as to whether they wished to join the British Army, as the decision to do so was made entirely voluntary. Of the four regiments one battalion (4/2 GR) opted *en masse* to join the Indian Army and became part of the 8th Gurkha Rifles as their 5th Battalion and is presently on their strength as 5/8 GR. In the event, large numbers of men from the 7th Gurkha Rifles and the 10th Gurkha Rifles, which recruited predominantly from Eastern Nepal, opted to join the Indian Army as against the British Army to whom their regiments were alloted. So, in order to retain a contingent from this area of Nepal, the Indian Army made the decision to re-raise the 11th Gorkha Rifles. Incidentally the Rais and Limbus are considered to be the most short tempered, fierce and sturdy amongst the hill warrior tribes. The

Kirantis dominate even the traditional Nepalese Army and the British Army as well.

The 11 Gorkha Rifles was officially re-raised on January 1, 1948, with the regimental centres at Palampur and Santa Cruz, Mumbai the regimental centre was subsequently shifted to Jalapahar in Darjeeling, then moved to Lucknow where it was firmly established. The regiment was raised predominantly with the manpower from the non-optees of the 7th Gurkha Rifles and the 10th Gurkha Rifles. As the regiment was raised by the Indian Army after independence, it was decided not to retain the honours and traditions of the first 11th Royal Gurkha Rifles of the British Indian Army.

Today, the regiment has a total of six regular and one Territorial Army battalions. The regiment took part in all major military operations India has undertaken since independence including the 1947 India Pakistan War, 1948 Operation Polo, 1965 India Pakistan War, 1971 India Pakistan War, and in the.

In the Indo - Pakistani war of 1971 the 5th battalion was instrumental in liberating Bangladesh, in fact the battle honour Bogra and theater honour East Pakistan was bestowed to the 5th only. In the operations of East Pakistan, the 5th had secured the Bogra town for 20 mountain division, in one of the most daring operations Lt Teja Bedi had single-handedly captured the headquarters along with the Commanding Officer and RMO of the prestigious Baluch Regiment of East Pakistan, the regimental flag of 52 Baluch Regiment is still hung upside down in the officers mess of the 5th and is one of the prized possession. Soon after the war, General Gopal Gurunath Bewoor of the regiment was appointed Chief of Army Staff of the Indian Army. He held the post from January 15, 1973 to May 31, 1975.

During the 1999 Kargil Conflict Manoj Kumar Pandey received the Param Vir Chakra (PVC), which is India's highest military award.

The 3rd, 4th and the 5th battalions are the oldest battalions of the Regiment. However the 4th Battalion was disbanded subsequently. The 5th battalion retains the honour of producing the maximum numbers of Lieutenant Generals with in the Regiment. The regiment has won a Param Vir Chakra which was won by Lt Manoj Kumar Pandev of the 1st Battalion during the 1999 Kargil Conflict 1 Victoria Cross Ganju Lama, the highest gallantry award of the british army, 6 Military Crosses, 2 Mahavir Chakras, 3 Ashok Chakras Capt M B Rat 5th Battalion, Rfn Sal Bahadur and Capt Punit Nath Putt, 7 PVSMs, 9AVSMs, 11 VSMs, 11 Vir Chakras, 5 Shaurya Chakras and 35 Sena Medals.

The units of the Regiments have participated in a number of UN missions abroad. The regiment has following battalions:

- 1st battalion - 1/11 Gorkha Rifles
- 2nd battalion - 2/11 Gorkha Rifles
- 3rd battalion - 3/11 Gorkha Rifles (Shingo)
- 4th battalion - (disbanded)
- 5th Battalion - 5/11 Gorkha Rifles (Bogra) The battalion was raised on 1 May 1948 consisting the non optees of the 7th Gurkhas and 10th Gurkhas of the British army. The battalion activily participated in all the war the nation fought after the independence. The battalion has served in many parts of the country including Jammu and Kashmir and North Eastern Part of the country. Some of the most notable commanders of the battalion are:
- 6th battalion - 6/11 Gorkha Rifles
- 7th battalion - 7/11 Gorkha Rifles
- The 106 Territorial Army Battalion is located in Darjeeling in West Bengal.

Battle and Theatre Honours

The battle honours of the regiment are Bogra, East Pakistan 1971, Shingo River Valley, Jammu and Kashmir 1971 and Batalik, Op Viiay J&K 1999. Theater honours are East Pakistan 1971 Jammu and Kashmir and Kargil for Op Vijay 1999.

Ashok Chakra

- Capt M B Rai of 5th Battalion, Rifleman Sal Bahadur and 2nd Lt Puneet Nath Dutt.

11

GORKHAS AND MODERN INDIA

At the outset, let us be clear about two terms that are used almost synonymously: Gorkha and Nepali. Both Gorkh (Gorkha is the most popular variant) and Nepali attest to a particular Indian community resident along the northern sub-Himalayan belt from the river Sutlej to the Brahmaputra. The terms can be commonly used synonymously and only differ in their etymological roots. To compare, we have the terms British and English, which refer to the same people. One has political overtones, the other ethnic connotations.

The tendency to refer to themselves as Gorkha is rooted in the reputation for valour the community earned, initially in overrunning the whole of the Sub-Himalayan region. For the military man, it is a pride to be called a Gorkha. "Gorkha" thus gained ground as a martial term and remains so even today. The word Gorkha itself, some say, has its origin in the name of Gorakhnath, an Indian mystic of yore. "Gorakhnath ki Jai" was once the battle cry of the Gorkhas. Another explanation is that they are the protectors of the cow—*g rakshak.*

But away from the battlefield, in the world of art and culture, language and literature, the appropriate term is "Nepali". Nepali also connotes a citizen of Nepal, but the word widely implies the language and its speakers anywhere in the world notwithstanding their citizenship. A language may be spoken in more than one country. Not only foreign languages, bin even Indian languages are spoken in other countries, Bengali in Bangladesh, Tamil in Sri Lanka, Sindhi, Urdu and Kashmiri in Pakistan. So it is wrong to assume that the speaker's language signifies his nationality.

India is the melting pot of humanity of diverse origins, religions and languages. From prehistoric periods different races have followed different routes to immigrate to India and no single tribe deserves the exclusive description of being truly Indian. As a matter of fact, no tribe can be called the real autochthons of India, and no definite dateline can be fixed for designating a group of immigrants as Indians and other as non-Indians on a chronological bases.

It is great misconception on the part of some sections of Indian sociologists and even historians to identify the Gorkhas rather simplistically as aborigines of present-day Nepal. If we trace the origin of their history objectively, the Gorkhas are as much the aborigines of India. The entire race of the present Gorkha community is the product of a long assimilation process between two great racial groups. Indo-Aryans ana the Mongoloid Kirats. As a distinct linguistic group, they belong to both the Indo-Aryan and Tibeto-Burman groups. The assimilation between the Mongoloid racial group from the north and the Indo-Aryan group from the south and northwest of the Indian continent and also the birth of two religions, Hinduism and Buddhism, produced a distinct race with a common culture.

The scriptures (*Manusmriti* 10/12, *Bhagavat Purana* 3.19.21-24 *Mahabharata* 2.18-22 etc.) also testify to the existence of the *Khasas* (speakers of *Khaskura*, now Nepali) in India since prehistoric times.

That the Gorkhas are the aborigines of India can be corroborated by historical facts. The Lichhavis were the first people of Indian origin to settle down in the plains of present-day Nepal. Around the 2nd and 3rd Centuries, many Indian Gorkhas started migrating to Nepal from north India and settled in the plains of Nepal. Along with them, other communities of high Hindu caste also advanced north and created small principalities in that region.

However, it was only with the Muslim invasion of Indian subcontinent from the 11th to the 16th Centuries that large-scale migration began from the plains of India into the Terai and hills of Nepal to save their Hindu faith from Muslim influences. The wave of immigrants was basically from the elite of the far more complex political system of northern India. The ancestors of the Gorkha people were, thus, Indian immigrants, mostly royal families from Rajputana and their numerous followers who fled their country during the medieval period to escape Muslim domination. The Shah dynasty of Nepal, now ousted from power, belonged to Rajput stock.

However, many *Khasas* and Kirat Gorkhas who were less concerned with their religion and joined the armies of Mughal kings. Those who were recruited in the Mughal army in India were known as *Munglane,* and many others who enlisted themselves in Sikh Maharaja Ranjit Singh's army in Lahore were known as *Lahure.*

Nepal still calls the Indian Nepalis *munglane* and the Gorkha soldiers, *lahure,* irrespective of their homelands.

Clearly, much before Nepal took its present shape, the Nepali-speaking people had already spread over northern and north-eastern regions of what constitutes India today. It is also to be remembered that India had also not acquired its present political borders then as it was divided into a number of kingdoms with unstable frontiers.

The Anglo-Gorkha War

In 1742, Prithvinarayan Shah, of Indian Rajput origin, became the king of Gorkha, a state about 60 miles west of Kathmandu. He wanted to unify all the Himalayan territories into a single powerful state. He was aware of the expanding power of the British in India and he knew that after the downfall of the Mughal Empire in India, European colonial powers were anxious to gain control over Indian principalities. The Gorkha ruler knew that unless the resource-rich Nepal valley came under his rule, it would be practically impossible to consolidate the fragmented states against the British. Prithvinarayan Shah, therefore, concentrated his troops towards the east. The final victory in the unification of Nepal valley came in 1769.

Prithvinarayan Shah had faced a challenge from the British during his unification campaign. In 1767, when Prithvinarayan blockaded Nepal valley to ensure absolute control, the last ruler of Kathmandu, Jayaprakash Malla, sought help from the East India Company, then the dominant power in India. However, the 2,400-strong Indian troops under the leadership of Captain Kinlock were badly defeated in the foothills of Terai and compelled to retreat after suffering heavy losses. This was the first Anglo-Nepal encounter.

After the death of Prithvinarayan, his son Simhapratap Shah became the king, but he dies two years later and his infant son Ranbahadur Shah was made king of Nepal. His uncle, the regent Bahadur Shah began to expand the territories of Nepal. He ventured eastward, crossing the Mechi River and reached Sikkim. To the west, he annexed part of northern India comprising Kumaun, Garhwal, Dehradun and Simla.

In 1795, Ranbahadur Shah appointed Bhimsen Thapa as the prime minister of Nepal. Under the commandership of General Amar Singh Thapa on the western flank, the Gorkha troops crossed the river Sutlej and attacked the fortress of Kangra. The Gorkha assault was finally checked by Sikh ruler Ranjit Singh at Kangra.

After their victory in the Nepal valley, the Gorkha army had started to foray outwards in two directions: east and west; and south along the line of the Terai region adjoining Oudh, the northern part of current Uttar Pradesh. By 1782, on the eastern flank, the Gorkhas had crossed the river Kosi and reached the Teesta. The second phase of annexation started at the same time. Towards the west, Lamjung and Tanahu were annexed in 1782, the Kali-Gandaki basin in 1786, Jumla and Doti in 1789, Garhwal in 1804, and the portion between Jumla and Sutlej in 1806. In this way, between 1806 and 1815, the Gorkha power extended nearly 1,500 km. from the river Teesta in the east to Sutlej in the opposite direction. The East India Company was perturbed at the incursion of the Gorkhas into the region. Strategically, it was of the utmost necessity to keep the Sutlej and Kangra region in British control in order to service its line of action towards the western flank. The British asked for these areas to be returned, but the Gorkhas demurred. A war broke over the issue in November 1814.

The East India Company mounted a large offensive with 30,000 British and Indian men against the fewer than 10,000 Gorkhas. There was furious fighting, particularly on the main battlefields of Kangra fortress, Jaithak, Deothal, Kumaun, Garhwal and the Rispan-Nalapani fortress near Dehradun, during which the Gorkhas under Amar Singh Thapa won the respect of the British for their tenacity and bravery. In the battle for the Khalanga fort, the British General R. Gillespie was killed. The fort eventually fell after the British diverted a small stream, the only source of water for the fort. The story is told of less than 60 men and women emerging from the fort under the leadership of fort commander Balbhadra Kunwar, naked *khukuris* in their hands and boldly marching away, leaving more than 600 dead or injured inside.

By this time, Maharaja Ranjit Singh was so highly impressed by the tough fight put up by the Gorkhas in his Kangra expedition of 1809 that he was determined to recruit these intrepid fighters into his army. The British too wanted the Gorkhas in their forces. The belligerent commander Balbhadra Kunwar and his undaunted soldiers declined the Company's offer to join forces and decided instead to fight the British as part of the Sikh army. Ranjit Singh raised two battalions purely of Gorkhas under the command of Balbhadra. The Sikh army with the Gorkha contingents not only regained Brimbar, Rajauri and Kotla but also subdued Nurpur, Jaswan and Kangra valley. Balbhadra was killed during fighting in the Afghan war.

On the banks of river Rispana, the British erected a monument, perhaps the only of its kind in the world that pays respectful tributes to the two combatants in the battle for Khalanga. Twin concrete obelisks stand on a common base—one is dedicated to General Gillespie, his officers and soldiers and the other to Balbhadra Kunwar and his gallant Gorkhas. The epitaph reads as follows in typical British understanding of Indian nomenclature:

as a tribute of respect
for our gallant adversary
Balbudder
Commander of the fort and his brave Gorkhas
who were afterwards while in the service
of
Runjit Singh
shot down in their ranks
to the last man by
the Afghan artillery

A British soldier-poet, John Ship, who confronted the Gorkhas face to face in the war, summarizes the action in the following lines:

Anglo - Gorkha War 1814

I never saw more steadinesses
Or bravery exhibited in my life.
Run they would not and of death
They seemed to have no fear
Though their comrades were falling
Thick around them, as bold
For we were so near to know
That every shot of ours told.

On the far western flank General Amar Singh Thapa was exasperated with the Nepal durbar's political stance and was anxious about the future of his soldiers. Having got Nepal to agree on Gorkha soldiers serving in the British army, General David Ochterlony honourably set Amar Singh Thapa at large along with his trusted men. One of the most tragic heroes of history, the brave Gorkha general moved alone towards the high Himalayas. And far from the battlefields, he breathed his last near Gosainthan, on July 29, 1816, unseen and unsung.

On December 2, 1815, a treaty was signed at Sugauli between King Girvan Yuddha Vikram Shah of Nepal and the East India Company. This treaty is known as the 'Sugauli Sandhi'.

Under the terms of the treaty Nepal had to cede all the southern plains and the eastern hills to the East India Company in the following manner:

(i) The whole of the lowlands between rivers Kali and Rapti.

(ii) The whole of lowlands (with the exception of Bootwal Khass) lying between the river Kali and the Gandaki.

(iii) The whole of lowlands between the Gandaki and Kosi.

(iv) The whole of lowlands between the rivers Mechi and Teesta.

(v) All the territories within the hills eastward of the river Mechi, including the forts and lands of Nagari and the pass of Nagarkote leading from Morang, to the hills, together with the territories lying between the Pass and Nagari.

These areas acceded to British India comprise modern-day Darjeeling, Jalpaiguri and some parts of Cooch Behar extending up to Goalpara district of Assam, the vast area to the north of the river Ganges, including Garhwal and Kumaun, extending up to Chamba Bhumi.

In this way more than 7,000 sq. miles, comprising one-third of the present Nepal, was annexed into British India With the cession of these areas, the boundaries between India and Nepal and Sikkim became well defined.

With the accession of these vast chunks to British India, a large number of Gorkhas became defacto residents of India and the present generation of Gorkhas in India is the descendants of these people who became part of British India in 1815.

The act of annexation is still going on. In 1975, Sikkim became the 25th state of India and the Gorkhas living there became Indian citizens de-jure.

In the background of this history, we may conclude that the Gorkhas residing in different parts of India are aborigines and settlers or migrants. As respectful citizens of the country today, they are playing a constructive role in the nation building. Their commitment to the unity and integrity and the development and defence of the country cannot be ignored.

Gorkhas Get Recruited

On May 15, 1815, months before the Sugauli Treaty was signed, British General David Ochterlony concluded an agreement with the Nepalese durbar on inducting Gorkhas into the East India Company's forces. Consequent to this deal, around 4,650 Gorkha soldiers opted to join the British army. Only those troops loyal to General Amar Singh Thapa and 583 soldiers in Maharaja Ranjit Singh's personal army declined the invitation.

Soon after, the East India Company raised three native battalions. The 1st. Gorkha Rifles was raised at Sabathu near Simla on April 24, 1815 and was known then as King George Ill's Own Gorkha Rifles or the Malaun Regiment. It consisted of Kumauni and Garhwali soldiers who fought the British under Amar Singh Thapa at Malaun.

That same day, the 2nd Gorkha Rifles was raised at Nahan. It comprised the men of the same stock who were captured by the British army during the war and held in the camps of Sirmoor and Dehradun. The regiment was known as 2nd King Edward VII's Own Gorkha Rifles or Sirmoor Regiment.

A third regiment was raised that day, the 3rd Gorkha Rifles, at Almora. It was made up of the hill men who accepted service with British after the conquest of Kumaun. The regiment was then known as the 3rd Queen Alexandra's Own Gorkha Rifles.

After 42 years of recruiting for the first three regiments, the East India Company set up two more regiments in 1857, one at Pithoragarh as the Extra Gorkha Regiment (later renamed the Prince of Wales' Own Gorkha Rifles or the 4th GR). Recruits for this regiment mainly came from Bakloh near Dalhousie.

The 5th Gorkha Rifles was raised at Abbottabad, in the North West Frontier Province, on the border of Hazara. Recruitment drew on the populace of the hills of UP and HP.

A battalion comprising Gorkhas, Manipuris and Oriyas was existent in Cuttack since 1817. It was known as the Cuttack Legion. In 1902, it was renamed the 6th Gorkha Rifles. The same year, a regiment to be based at

Thayetmyo in Burma was set up and named the 7th GR. In Sylhet, now in Bangladesh, south of the Khasi-Jainta hills, a battalion called the Sylhet Local Battalion took in local youths. Later in 1903, given the number of the Gorkhas in its ranks, the Sylhet Local Battalion became the 8th GR.

The 9th GR was originally raised at Fatehgarh in UP early in 1817 as the Fatehgarh Levy. It was subsequently elevated to a regiment. Similarly, the 10th Gorkha Rifles was born in 1887 as the Military Police at Memyo in Burma and consisted of Gorkha and Garhwali troops. In 1892, it became the 1st Burma Rifles. In 1901, however, it was renamed the 10th GR, or the Princess Mary's Own Gorkha Rifles.

The British Government raised the final Gorkha regiment, the 11th GR, during World War I. It had four battalions composed of Gorkha soldiers drawn from other Gorkha regiments, but was disbanded after the war. It was resurrected by India at the time of the 1948 war with Pakistan.

Early Gorkha Societies

It is incorrect to infer historically that the Gorkhas are late migrants to India. There are records of their presence in the country since the days of the Mughals. During the monarchy of Prithvinarayan Shah (1743-75), some families were banished from the kingdom on account of their conversion to Christianity and they fled to India and settled in Gaya. For eons, Gorkhas considered Banaras as a place of salvation and centre of education. The Nepalese who resided in the land of the Mughals were, and are still, called *munglane*.

Of course, after the treaty of 1815 the number of Gorkhas in India increased in big numbers due mainly to the open recruitments in army and as sentries in coal and oil fields, in tea and cinchona plantations, for road construction and tree felling The Gorkhas, over time, could be found in substantial number in north India from Kashmir to Manipur.

The Northeast: A large number of Gorkhas have been residents in the north-east region of India for over a century and a half. Many Gorkhas were inducted into the Assam Light Infantry. This had been formed in Cuttack in 1817 and was then transferred to Assam. The British granted the Gorkhas, who reached the Northeast as members of different regiments over a period of time, land and facilities so that even after retirement, they would have a pool of Gorkhas from which to draw recruits for their army.

Assam: The historical name of Assam is Kamarup. In the Puranic Age, Nepal and Kamarup comprised a single domain. Matsyendranath, a great mystic yogi of Kamarup, is said to have gone to Nepal and settled there. This ancient link between Nepal and Assam was resurrected in modern times in the 19th Century. In the early days, the Gorkhas were cattle herders in the Assam valley, their grazing grounds spread from Baralimara to Bhavani Devithan. Bura Chapari of Tezpur was declared a professional grazing reserve in 1881. In 1920, the Gorkhas were ordered to vacate the land, but, after public pressure, the order was repealed in 1933.

After the success of tea gardens in Assam, the Assam Company began bringing in labourers from 1853. After passing several legislations in 1863, people from Nepal and other communities were given the freedom to enter the tea plantation in Assam. The Gorkha population in Assam naturally went up.

Labour was hired not only in tea gardens but in the other fields also. In 1889, oil was explored at Digboi. Gorkhas were employed from the very beginning of the enterprise. Since the native people feared to enter the dense forest of Digboi., the British employed the Nepalese for the operational work. Places surrounding Digboi, like Itabhatti, Rasthpati, Nalapatti, Muliabari, Topabasti,

Agreement Line, Goru Phatak were all originally inhabited by Gorkhas. During World War I, when the native people fled from Digboi, the Gorkhas were appointed as security personnel at the oilfields. In 1923, Jitbahadur Pradhan was authorized to recruit labourers for the refineries. He brought in hundreds of Nepali workers, particularly from North Bengal.

Nagaland: In Nagaland, Hari Prasad Gorkha Rai, an authority on the Gorkha community in the Northeast, written about how 400 hundred years ago, some men of Chiechama village were going to their fields when they came across three young, tired and hungry Gorkha boys. The villagers took pity on them and brought them home. Two of the boys died of cholera. The one who survived said his name was 'Rai'. A villager elder adopted him and later even married him off to his daughter. In course of time, Rai became assimilated into the Angami tribe and his descendents are now called Metha Tophris, or non-Angami Methama clan. Till today, it is a custom to give a male child in the clan the name 'Rayi'. This commemorates the name of the clan's original father. If this story is true, then the history of the Gorkhas in Nagaland begins in the early 17th Century.

In the compound of the 3rd Assam Rifles at Kohima, Nagaland's capital, there is a memorial stone that places the date of the base's establishment in 1835. This means the Gorkhas have been in Nagaland since then. When the British marched in soldiers from the Native Infantry Cachar Levy and Artillery Force to Kohima, they stayed back and were rehabilitated at Chanmari.

Manipur: The entry of the Nepalis and their settlement in Manipur can be traced to 1819 at the earliest. It is quite probable that some scattered Nepali families were already settled in Manipur before this date. Some scholars push back the history of the Gorkhas in Manipur to the beginning of the 16th Century. Lore also has it that the first Nepali came to Manipur at the beginning of the

10th Century. He married a Meitei girl called Kumbi, who belonged to the Mayang Heikong Ningol, a popular Manipuri clan. Since this man reared cows and buffaloes in the *Khuti,* or the *goth* (cowshed), his descendants are knowns as gotimayan.

The first batch of Gorkhas came to Manipur during the time of Raja Gambhir Singh. In 1824, the Gorkhas of the 16th Sylhet Local Battalion, later to become the 8th Gorkha Rifles, were included in the Police Levy of Gambhir Singh. During the first quarter of the 19th Century, Manipur was much troubled by Burmese intruders and troops. To secure Manipur, Gambhir Singh raised an army in 1825 and recruited Gorkhas from Sylhet for it. The militia was named the 'Victoria Paltan'. The nomenclature is a clear indication of the preponderance of Gorkhas in the army since the word *paltan* is a Nepali corruption of the English 'platoon'. Having earned the trust of the British, Gorkha soldiers were detailed to protect all the Political Agents. They were also brought in as cooks, milkmen, traders and agriculturists.

The number of Gorkha soldiers in Manipur increased when the East India Company moved the 23rd, 43rd and 44th battalions of the 8th Gorkha Rifles to Manipur around 1880. Later, according to the records of the Chief Commissioner of Assam, 400 Gorkha soldiers from Golaghat and 200 from Silchar were brought in. In 1891, more were relocated to the region from other places in Assam. Maharaja Chandrakriti's reign too saw many Gorkhas coming in.

At the beginning of the 20th Century, Gorkhas were being recruited in the Assam Military Police, where 82 of them were posted at Tura in the Garo Hills Battalion, 730 were at Dibrugarh in the Lakhimpur Battalion, 331 at Kohima in the Naga Hills Battalion, 111 at Silchar in the Silchar Battalion, and 105 at Dhaka in the Dhaka Battalion.

In 1915, the 2nd Gorkha Rifles stationed at Imphal

was replaced by the Darang Military Police when the renowned fighters were deployed for action somewhere in Europe. This very Darang Military Police stationed at Manipur was converted into the 4th Assam Rifles in 1917 and 80 per cent of its personnel comprised Gorkhas.

Almost all the Gorkhas who came to Manipur on active service settled there permanently after retirement. The British government allotted land to the personnel of the 4th Assam Rifles first in Thangmaiband and later in special colonies in Eroisembe, Chink, Tangri, Kalapahar, Torbung, Maram, Imphal, Irang and Kanglatombi. After 1945, many personnel from Subhas Chandra Bose's INA also made Manipur their home.

The fact that Nepali literature's first poetical work in print came from Manipur is proof that the Gorkhas were fully assimilated into Manipur society and its social pursuits by 1894, the year that Tulachand Alay wrote and published *Manipurko Sawai.*

Mizoram: The Gorkhas have been in Mizoram at least for a century and a half In 1865, Colonel T.H. Lewin wrote, "I had formed a high opinion of the little Gurkhas, who under Col. Macpherson, had done the fighting of the expedition, and I obtained permission to send to Nepal and get immigrants from there to colonize this frontier waste." Gorkha colonies were established on the Myani river, a northern affluent of the Karnaphuli, now in Bangladesh. Colonel Lewin wanted to establish a number of villages along the "frontier waste" between the plains and the hills so that a well-defined boundary between the local and British territories could be established. Colonel Lewin records that "the country where the villages were located had previously been uninhabited, for fear of the marauding Lushais, and my idea had been to establish there a good stockade villages of courageous, stiff-people like the Gurkhas, who should serve as the buffer between the Mong Raja's territory and the independent Lushais to the east."

After the construction of stockades at Lungai and Aizawl, peace was restored in most of the hills. The government needed man-power—traders, masons, dak-runners, chowkidars, farmers and others—for which they turned to the Gorkhas, fearing that the natives were not yet fully docile. The Gorkhas also reached Mizoram as personnel of the Frontier Police Battalion. It is also recorded that by 1891, hundreds of people freely moved across the frontiers of Manipur and Chittagong hill tracts. The Gorkhas were not among them, however. They were imported by the British themselves. There is a case recorded in 1872 when the Gorkhas rescued the kidnapped Mary Winchester, daughter of the manager of the Alexandrapore Tea Garden, from the hands of Lushai chieftains. This act of loyalty won the Gorkhas the trust of the British, who recommended that they settle in the area for good.

The Surma Valley Military Police Battalion, later known as 1st Assam Rifles, was raised at Changsil in the north Lushai Hills by General Tregears in 1889. Its ranks were mainly filled by Gorkha soldiers. The Gorkhas, after their retirement from the army and the police forces, accepted the Lushai Hills as their homeland. Today, they form the most socially organized Gorkha community in north-east India.

Meghalaya: The primal settlement of the Nepalis in Meghalaya, once called the Khasi-Jaintia Hills, can be dated to the establishment of their social organizations there—the Gorkha Thakurbari (1824), Gorkha Durga Puja Committee (1872) and Gorkha Union (1886). The Thakurbari certainly from records appears to be the oldest organization of Gorkhas in the whole of the Northeast. It still runs two temples and one middle school for girls. The Gorkha Durga Puja Committee was started by the Gorkhas of the 1st and 2nd battalions of 8 GR. In 1940, when the platoon was shifted to Quetta, now in Pakistan, the committee was handed over to the civilians and ex-servicemen residing in and around Shillong. Another older organisation is the Gorkha Union, later known as the Gorkha Association.

The history of 8th Gorkha Rifles reveals a lot about the Nepalis in Meghalaya. Major Alban Wilson writes: "In 1845, an outpost of the regiment was established at Umbai in the Khasi Hills, under the command of Subedar Deoraj Alay, who was given the civil powers of a third class magistrate. He died after he had been two years at Umbai, Cherrapunji, but in that short time, he had endeared himself so much to the inhabitants that they erected a large tomb over his grave by the road side, and to the present day, every inhabitant of the place worships at his grave, and when passing by, places a chew of *supari* on it."

In 1866, Lieutenant W.J. Williamson was appointed the commissioner of Garo Hills. He set up a police force in Tura comprising two inspectors, two sub-inspectors, six head constables and 100 constables. Most of the constables and coolies brought to Tura were Gorkhas from Goalpara in Assam. In an entry in his diary on December 25, 1867, Williamson notes, "... The Nepalee coolies and the constables worked quite to my satisfaction...." The Nepalis were employed in trees felling and road construction also. When the American missionaries reached Garo Hills, they had taken 12 Gorkhas with them from Dhubri in Assam. AG. Phillips wrote in his diary on December 12, 1876: "I am at Tura at last. I left Goalpara November Seventh, reaching Dhubri on the following day, where I stopped to get coolies for building, as this is a place to which many Nepalese come seeking work."

When one goes through the history of the 8 GR, Shillong of 1867 could not have shown any resemblance to the charming cantonment and civil station that so many subsequently came to know it as. Asked what the place was like when he marched into Shillong with the 44th battalion of 8 GR, Captain Kalu Thapa replied, "There was not a rat there."

Along with the servicemen, Gorkhas were "invited" to rear cattle in the Northeast. Lyndred Shira, a writer based in Tura, discloses this in the following words: "When Tura was first occupied by the American Baptist Mission in 1876, there was hardly anything out here. The present site of the school was a thick jungle, infested with wild and dreaded elephants that roamed at large breaking the silence of the atmosphere with their vocal trumpets. Goshai, a Nepali fellow, must have occupied this plot of land sometimes towards the beginning of this century. He must have been invited by the British Government to start a cattle farm here, purposely for supply of milk to the residents of the locality." Goshai's grazing farm was known, till late, as *Nippal adding*, or 'Nepali hill'.

In 1872, Shillong had 1,363 inhabitants, 935 in the active service. Of those in the services, 772 were Gorkhas. By now, The Nepalis had made homes in almost all the places of Meghalaya, though there was no single area inhabited fully by them.

Manorath Upadhya, a third grade 'jemadar' of the Garo Hills Military Police Battalion, wrote *Tirthavali* in 1915. As in Manipur, this once again testifies to the social and literary pursuits of the Gorkhas living with the Garos and Khasis from very early on.

Sikkim, Darjeeling and Dooars: The history of Sikkim, Darjeeling and the Dooars is interwoven due to their social, cultural and geographical homogeneity. The frontiers of these lands have undergone many changes as has their ownership.

Sikkim: The early history of Sikkim is shrouded in the thick mist of the legends of the Lepchas, considered the aboriginals of this region. The first known raja of Sikkim, Khey Bumsa of Tibetan origin, settled in Sikkim with Chumbi Valley as his capital. He maintained friendly ties with the Lepchas. His grandson, Guru Tashi, shifted the capital to Gangtok. Guru Tashi's grandson Phuntsog

Namgyal was the first consecrated king of Sikkim and the first to set up a centralized government. The kingdom was many times its size today. In the north it touched Phari in Tibet, in the east Paro in Bhutan, in the south Titalya near the borders of Bihar and Bengal and in the west, the Tamor River in Nepal. Phuntsog moved the capital to Yuksum, as it was a more central place to rule from. His son Tenzing Namgyal shifted the capital to Rapdantse. When Tenzing died in 1700, Chhador, the son from his second Tibetan wife, succeeded his father. But Pedi Wangmo, the first heir from the king's first Bhutanese wife, opposing the succession, invited a force from Bhutan. The Rapdantse palace was captured and held by the Bhutanese for eight years. On the mediation of the Tibetan government, Bhutan withdrew its force, but areas in the south-east, Kalimpong and Rhenock remained Bhutanese possession.

Earlier in 1780, during the reign of Phuntsog Namgyal, the Gorkhas made incursions and took over Ilam and Taplejung and advanced up to west Sikkim. By 1814, the Gorkhas had captured the whole of the lower hills and Terai region between the Mechi and Teesta rivers. The East India Company was also eyeing the Himalayan region of the north and the growing ascendancy of the Gorkhas came in its way. The British assumed that without their intervention, the Gorkhas would turn the whole of Sikkim and the hills south and west of the Teesta into a province of Nepal. So in the guise of extending a hand of peace to Sikkim, the British concluded a treaty at Titalya in 1817 under which the whole of the territory between the Mechi and the Teesta, a tract extending 4,000 sq. miles ceded by Nepal under the treaty of Sugauli, was given to Sikkim. The gifted portion included the present Darjeeling district. The operating portions of the treaty were:

Article I: 'The Honorable East India Company cedes, transfers and makes over in full sovereignty to the Sikkimputtee Rajah, his heirs or successors, all the hilly or mountainous country situated to the eastward of the Mechi river and to the westward of the Teesta river, formerly possessed by the Raja of Nepaul but ceded to the Honorable East India Company by the treaty of peace signed at Segaulee."

Article VIII: "The Honorable East India Company guarantees to the Sikkimputtee Rajah and his successors, the full and peaceable possession of the tract of hilly country specified in the First Article of the present Agreement."

Ten years after the treaty was signed, a dispute arose between Sikkim and Nepal, which according to the terms of treaty, were referred to the East India Company. In 1928, Captain Lloyd was deputed to effect a settlement. Accompanied by with J. W. Grant, Lloyd penetrated the hills, which was still a terra incognita to the British, as far as Rinchinpong. It was this journey that opened up the eyes of the British to Darjeeling.

Darjeeling: In February 1929, Lloyd reached 'the Old Goorka Station' called Darjeeling and remained there for six days. In his report, he claims that he was the first European to have visited the place and "was immediately struck with its being well adapted for the purpose of a sanatorium". He further adds, 'Should the climate prove too cold, Ging which is below it, and to which there is very easy access, would remedy the evil." On all grounds he strongly urged the importance of securing possession of the place for the British, and in particular, pointed out its advantages as a centre that would facilitate trade, and as a position of great strategic importance, commanding as it did, the entrance into Nepal and Bhutan.'

Darjeeling itself, though formerly occupied by a large village and the residence of one of the principal Kazis, was deserted, and the country around it was sparsely inhabited; but Lloyd says in his report, 'If this part of the hills was resumed by us, or ceded, the Chief and the people who have emigrated would instantly return." At the same time, Grant also impressed on the Governor-General, Lord William Bentinck, the numerous advantages promised by the establishment of a sanatorium in Darjeeling, and strongly advocated its occupation for military purposes.

These representations were not neglected by Lord Bentinck, who promptly deputed Captain Herbert to examine the country in company with Grant. The report of these two gentlemen conclusively proved the feasibility of establishing a sanatorium at Darjeeling. They also suggested that Darjeeling might prove a valuable depot for European recruits, and even a permanent cantonment for a European regiment. Accordingly, Lloyd was directed to open negotiations with the Raja of Sikkim for the cession of Darjeeling in return for an equivalent in money or land. The negotiations ended in the execution by Raja of Sikkim of a deed of grant on February 1, 1835. The deed, which is commendably short, runs as follows:

> "The Governor-General having expressed his desire for the possession of the hill of Darjeeling on account of its cool climate, for the purpose of enabling the servants of his Government, suffering from sickness, to avail themselves of its advantages, I, the Sikkimputtee Rajah, out of friendship for the said Governor-General, hereby present Darjeeling to the East India Company, that is all land south of the Great Runjeet River, east of the Balasun, Kahaif and Little Runjeet rivers, and west of the Rungno and Mahanuddi rivers."

This was an unconditional cession, but in 1841 the Government granted the Raja an allowance of Rs 3,000 as compensation, and raised the grant to Rs 6,000 in 1846.

By 1840, the incursion into the hilly territory was well under way and a road had been built from Pankhabari; a hotel had been opened up in Kurseong and a second in Darjeeling. In Darjeeling, some 30 private houses had been built and nearly as many as more locations had been taken up at Lebong. But development projects suffered for lack of manpower since the raja of Sikkim had prohibited his subjects from going to Darjeeling and helping in establishing the new settlements. The Company proposed various expedients to populate Darjeeling. They invited the Lepcha refugees who had been forced by the oppression of the raja to flee from Darjeeling to Nepal, they imported labourers from the indigo plantation of Rampur and Ramgarh, i.e., Gaya and Hazaribagh in Bihar, and procured settlers from Nepal and Bhutan.

In the mean time, the relations between Sikkim and the Company were far from satisfactory. Namgay Dewan, the administrator of Sikkim, was not pleased at the British occupation of Darjeeling. He discouraged in every way the migration of people of Sikkim to Darjeeling. The Dewan proved uncongenial to the British. Bad blood reached a climax in November 1849, when Sir Joseph Hooker and Dr Campbell, were suddenly seized and made prisoners while travelling m Sikkim. Though they were released the following month, an avenging force crossed the Great Rangit into Sikkim in February 1850. They camped on the bank of the river for some weeks, but were recalled without any further demonstration. The British forced the raja to sign a treaty under which, as a penalty, the grant of Rs 6,000 per annum that the raja was receiving since 1846, was withdrawn. The king was further punished by the annexation of the Sikkim Terai which he had received as a gift from the British and which was the only lucrative and fertile land he possessed. At the same time, there was annexed to it the portion of the Sikkim hills bounded by the Rammam on the north, the Great Rangit and the Teesta and Nepal border on the west. The result was to confine Sikkim to the mountainous hinterland and to cut off all the access to the plains. The annexation was profitable in kind also as it only involved the payment of a small tax to the treasury at Darjeeling.

The Kalimpong tract was taken from Bhutan in 1865 and was added to the district of Darjeeling. This was the last addition to the district, which then acquired its present dimensions.

Dooars: The Bhutanese were constantly engaged in aggression in the eastern frontiers and there were apprehensions about an attack on Darjeeling. In 1863, Sir Ashley Eden was sent to Bhutan with a proposal of conciliation. But the Bhutan government not only rejected the overture, it also openly insulted the envoy at the durbar and incarcerated him. However, Ashley freed himself and fled from Punakha, the then capital of Bhutan, and reached Darjeeling in April 1864. After further fruitless negotiations, the British determined to annex the Bengal Dooars and much of the hill territory, including the forts of Dalingkot, Pasaka and Diwangiri into the district of Darjeeling and the plains. A military force of sufficient strength was accordingly dispatched to Bhutan. The fortresses were captured and the whole of the Dooars was completely occupied by the middle of January 1865. On November 11, 1865, a treaty was executed at Sinchula. Article II of the treaty reads:

> "Whereas in consequence of repeated aggressions of the Bhootan Government and of the refusal of that Government to afford satisfaction for those aggressions, and of their insulting treatment of the officers sent by his Excellency the Governor-General in Council for the purpose of procuring an amicable adjustment of differences existing between the two states, the British Government has been compelled to seize by an armed force the whole of the Dooars and certain Hill Posts protecting the passes into Bhootan, and whereas the Bhootan Government has now expressed its regret for past misconduct and a desire for the

> establishment of friendly relations with the British Government, it is hereby agreed that the whole of the tract known as the Eighteen Dooars, bordering on the districts of Rungpoor, Cooch Behar, and Assam, together with the Talook of Ambaree Fallacottah and the Hill territory on the left bank of the Teesta up to such points as may be laid down by the British Commissioner appointed for the purpose is ceded by the Bhootan Government to the British Government for ever."

Out of eighteen Dooars, 11 are collectively called the Assam Dooars and seven as the Bengal Dooars. Till 1864, the tract from Ambari and Falakata to the Seven Dooars, i.e., Ghurkhola, Banska, Chhappa Goonee, Chhappa Khamar, Bijnee, Bun Goma and Kuling were within the territories of the Raja of Sikkim and Raja of Coochbehar. Later, taking the Seven Dooars and carving out a portion of Coochbehar, the district of Jalpaiguri was formed. The demography of this area is different to that of the rest of West Bengal. Here the bulk of population comprises Gorkhas, and Koches and Meches, i.e., the aboriginal Rajbansis. After the launching of tea plantations in the Dooars, many more labourers from Bihar, Chhotanagpur and Chhattisgarh were inducted into the workforces. It is interesting to note that their lingua franca is Nepali.

Himamhal Pradesh: The settlement of the Gorkhas in Himanchal Pradesh has a history of nearly 250 years. Between 1803 and 1814, the Gorkha Empire included the swathe from Kangra to Srinagar. After nearly 12 years of rule here, under the treaty of Sugauli in 1815, Nepal had to cede Simla, Kumaun, Garhwal and all the low lands lying between the Chenab and the Sunkosh, north of the river Ganga. The majority of the Gorkhas settled in the district of Kangra, Dharamshala and Bakloh, near Dalhousie in Chamba district. These people cannot be categorized as migrants in any way since they merged into India with the lands they lived on. The 1st Gorkha Rifles was raised at Sabathu near Simla in 1815 and it was given a permanent location at Dharamshala. The first regular settlement of the Gorkhas in Dharmashala is known to have taken place some time between 1879 and 1882. Gorkha army pensioners lived in Chilghari. At present, they have settled in many villages, such as Ramnagar, Shyamnagar, Dan, Sidh Ban, Sadar Ghaniyara, Yol, Dal, Tota Rani, Chandmani and Chani.

About the earliest settlement of Gorkhas in Kangra district, it is said that some families settled in the village of Sahaura near Kangra during the seizure of the Kangra fort from 1805 to 1809. Many Gorkha families settled down in villages around Malaun fort after its fall, and one of the prominent families was that of the forefathers of Arjun Singh Bista, a former legislator from Nalagarh.

One of the oldest associations of Gorkhas in Dharamshala is the Himachal Punjab Gorkha Association, established in 1916. The main objective of the association was to render financial help to widows, orphans and destitutes, stipend to poor students, preservation of the Gorkha's language and culture and seeking government assistance to benefit and create employment for the Gorkha pensioners.

Uttarakhand: The history of Gorkha settlement in Uttaranchal, the erstwhile northern Uttar Pradesh, is as old as that of Himachal Pradesh.

The districts of Kumaun and Garhwal fell under the Gorkha kingdom between 1790 and 1815. Dehradun valley was captured by Balbhadra Kunwar in 1803. General Amar Singh Thapa was in charge of Kumaun and Garhwal, whereas Balbhadra Kunwar was the administrator of the Dehradun valley. Srinagar and Simla were under the charge of Bahadur Bhandari and Dasharath Khatri. Ranjor Thapa, the son of Amar Singh Thapa, was entrusted with Sirmoor in Himachal Pradesh. After the Anglo-Gorkha War, when these lands were ceded to British India, the soldiers and the settlers of these places became de facto subject of India.

After the treaty of 1815, the 2nd GR and the 3rd GR were raised in Sirmoor and Almora respectively. The retired soldiers of these regiments were later rehabilitated by the British, who set up colonies and provided lands in Nalapani, Raipur, Killagarh, Gorapur Estate, Navada, Garhi, Dakra Bazar, Lachhiwala, Vizpur, Anarwala, Ghuchukpani, Chandrabani, Parade Ground, Paltan Bazar and Phaltu Line.

The people resident in these areas, which now make up parts of Uttarakhand, have done well in many spheres. Their intellect and intrepidity have also blazed a trail in the annals of the Indian Gorkhas. It was Dehradun that established the All India Gorkha League in 1925. Thakur Chandan Singh was its founder president. The League, a socio-political organisation, fought for the rights of the Gorkhas through its two Nepali journals, *Gorkha Sansar* (1926) and *Tarun Gorkha* (1928). Chandan Singh also edited the *Great Himalayan,* an English journal from 1926. The All India Gorkha League came to a halt after 1934, succumbing to pressures from the British administration. Again, it is Dehradun that raised the first voice for the recognition of Nepali language in the Indian constitution. Anand Singh Thapa, the editor of *Jagrat Gorkha,* wrote a memorandum to the President of India to this end in 1956, a call that was later taken up by other establishments there and in other parts of India.

Poet Gumani Panta of Almora (1790-1887), lyrist Bahadur Smgh Baral of Kangra (b.1893), music maestro Mitrasen Thapa of Dharamshala (1892-1947), national poet Gopal Singh Nepali (1911-64), et al, hailed from Uttarakhand. Being the land of Amar Singh Thapa and Veer Balbhadra, innumerable soldiers born here have served the country. Martyrs like Major Durga Malla and Captain Dalbahadur Thapa of the INA belonged to this region. The first Gorkha General, Omkar Singh Bhandari, Param Vir Chakra winner Dhansingh Thapa and a host of gallantry award recipients have done the Indian Army proud.

Unifying Force

It seems the Gorkhas are born to fight for the unification of a country. First they fought under Prithvinarayan Shah and conquered Baisi and Chaubisi, or the 22 and 24 states lying between the Kali and the Mechi rivers, and thus unified Nepal. Then, post the 1815 Treaty of Sugauli, the Gorkhas became friends with the British in bringing about changes that made India the territorial entity it is today.

When the East India Company came to India, the country was a mosaic of small princely states. In 1815, three Gorkha regiments were raised and these regiments pioneered the process of unifying India. Two years later in 1817, the Gorkhas helped the East India Company annex Bombay. In 1825-26, they subdued Bharatpur. Sind was brought under British India in 1839 and the Punjab in 1846. It was a big irony of the battlefield that during the first Anglo-Sikh war, the British and Gorkhas had to fight face-to-face against the Sikhs and Gorkhas, an instance of loyalty above community. The British forces annexed Oudh, Jhansi, Ajmer, Bhopal, Jaipur, Satara and many more independent princely states. It was the Gorkhas that brought the tribal lands of the whole of the Northeast under British India. Similarly, Burma was won in 1852. Even after winning independence, the Gorkha regiments overcame the bifurcation of the Gorkha forces between Britain and India to unite Andaman-Nicobar islands with India. Kashmir and Hyderabad were not parts of India till 1947. Forty thousand Gorkhas were deployed there to bring them into the Indian domain. The process of consolidation is going on. Only in 1975, the state of Sikkim, of its own, became a part of India.

In 1885, the Indian National Congress was formed under the leadership of Allan Octavian Hume. Hume treated the party as a 'safety-valve' whereas the Congress wanted to use him as the 'lightning-conductor' to solve the various politico-socio-economic problems facing India.

The second session of the Indian National Congress was held in Calcutta in 1886 and the third in Madras in 1887. Up to the third session of Congress, no one suspected it of any illegal activities, but subsequently a special branch of police was created to follow the party's activities.

The partition of Bengal and the Swadeshi movement divided the Congress into the moderate and extremist groups. The latter mainly operated from Bengal, Bombay and the Punjab. In Bengal, Aurobindo Ghose was the head of the extremists. In 1907, an attempt was made on the life of Kingsford, the Calcutta Presidency magistrate. The following year, Khudiram Bose and Prafulla Chaki were put to death for the act.

In 1907, a number of revolutionary magazines were published from the different parts of the country. From Bengal *Bande Mataram, Jugantar, Howrah Hitaishi, Gorkha Sathi* and others were published. The editor of the Nepali magazine, Gorkha Sathi was Pritiman Thapa and the publisher was Han Singh Thapa. It was published from Calcutta in 1907.

Pritiman Thapa was a patriot who fought against the British rule in India. He gave a call to Gorkha soldiers to fight against the British in India.

Regarding Thapa's acts, the Commissioner of Police in Calcutta sent a telegram to the Director of Criminal Intelligence on May 28, 1907. It reads:

> "A Nepalese, Prithiman Thapa, addresses a meeting at Calcutta Square, 27th. Evening, about 200 present, advocated publishing monthly newspapers for distribution to Gorkha soldiers to ascertain situations and their duties for the motherland, case of poverty in India and true connection between Gorkhas and Bengalese and English. Unfortunately Nepali gentleman visiting Calcutta found difficulty in mixing with Bengalese

> not knowing Bengali. He will strive to bring Bengalese and Nepalese together...." *(Foreign Dept. External IB Proceedings, Sept. 1907, Nos. 101-9, National Archives of India)*

This simple act of reminding the Gorkha soldiers of their duty to India was the humble beginning of the community's active participation in the early phase of the freedom movement.

Non-Cooperation Movement: The Non-Cooperation Movement was first adopted at a special session of the Congress that was held in September 1920 in Calcutta under the able leadership of Mahatma Gandhi and was reaffirmed at the annual session at Nagpur in December 1920. As part of this movement, people were asked to renounce government titles, to boycott governmental and educational institutions, legislatives, law courts, foreign goods and to refuse to pay taxes, etc.

The Gorkhas who took part in the Non-Cooperation Movement from Darjeeling district in Bengal were Dal Bahadur Giri, Partiman Singh Lama, Savitri Devi, Putalimaya Poddar, Agam Singh Giri, Man Bahadur Giri, Bhagat Bir Tamang and a host of others.

Dal Bahadur Giri was a veteran freedom fighter of national level. His political career began from Sikkim where he was a head clerk in the Royal Palace, and was deported from the state by the king under the influence of British officials. He returned to Darjeeling in 1916. At the time the whole country had plunged headlong into the struggle for independence under the leadership of Mahatma Gandhi. After the passage of the Rowlatt Act, Pandit Shyam Sundar Chakravarty, one of the greatest leaders of anti-partition movement of Bengal, was arrested under the Defence of India Act and interned at Kalimpong for a period of four years. Dal Bahadur Giri came in close contact with him there. The anti-British spirit that was burning in his mind became flame under the influence of Pandit Shyam Sundar, who advised him to join the Congress and serve the country.

In 1917, the All India Congress Committee Session was held in Calcutta, presided over by Mrs Annie Besant. Dal Bahadur Giri went with Dr Charu Chandra Sanyal, a prominent Congress leader of North Bengal, to Calcutta to attended the Session. There he met Janakinath Ghosal and Deshbandhu Chittaranjan Das. None from Darjeeling had ever attended a Congress session before Giri. After becoming the first, Giri missed no other session in his life.

In 1918, the Congress conference was held in Delhi under the presidentship of Madan Mohan Malaviya. Dalbahadur Giri was, as usual, a participant. On the last day of the conference, Gandhiji, taking a personal interest in Giri, called him and had a conversation with the Gorkha leader. Back home in Darjeeling, Giri became an ardent follower of Gandhiji and dedicated himself to freeing India from the British. The following year, Dalbahadur Giri attended the Congress Session of Bombay and in 1920 he attended the Nagpur Session, from where he brought membership forms, receipt books and other literature of the Congress party. He then established a Congress branch office at Pedong, a small town bordering Sikkim and Darjeeling. This propelled his political activities. He began showing the charkha and takli to Gorkha volunteers.

In 1921, the then Deputy Commissioner of Darjeeling, S. W. Goode, organized a public meeting at what is now the Rink cinema hall, to mobilize public opinion against the Non-Co-operation movement launched by Gandhiji. Admission at the meeting was strongly regulated by invitation cards. Dal Bahadur Giri was deliberately not invited. But Giri was determined to be at this gathering of the town elite. Using the card issued to Partiman Singh Lama, he managed to get into the meeting hall. Discarding the ordinary norms of a public meeting and to the surprise of all, Goode took the chair himself. Dal

Bahadur Giri jumped on his chair and protested against such an act of the DC. The British and their supporter tried to silence him and drive him out of the meeting, but a sardar from a local tea garden cautioned them against physically throwing Giri out. Goode had to leave the hall from a door at the rear. Jangbir Sapkota, another stalwart present there, openly appreciated the stand of Giri in the auditorium itself.

The Deputy Commissioner was annoyed by Giri's audacity. He issued an order for Giri to leave the town immediately. But Giri replied, "I will not leave my motherland even if death comes." Gin was arrested on June 27, 1921 on charges of anti-government activities.

Giri was arrested and jailed for the second time in November, 1921. He was then arranging a meeting at Chowk Bazar in Darjeeling to protest the arrest of Mahatma Gandhi, Muhammad Ali and Shaukat Ali in Waltier. This time he was not kept in the Darjeeling jail but was dispatched to the Hoogly jail. From Hoogly he was transferred to Berhampore Central jail, where Subhas Chandra Bose was also confined. They were known to each other. While in jail, Bose fell ill and was sent to Calcutta. The health of Dalbahadur Giri too was in a precarious condition. He was suffering from tuberculosis. Sensing his last days were near, he was released from jail. Frail and weakened he came to Darjeeling and breathed his last in 1924 at the age of just 36.

On his death, Gandhiji wrote in his *Young India* of November 13, 1924:

> "Many readers of *Young India* know Sjt. Dalbahadur Giri by name only. Some may not have even heard his name. Yet he was one of the bravest of national workers. As I am writing for *Young India* I have a wire from Kalimpong with the news of the death of this comparatively unknown patriot. I tender my condolence to his family. He was a cultured Gorkha and was doing good works among the

> Gorkhas in the nearby Darjeeling. During 1921, in common with the thousands, he was also imprisoned for the non-co-operation activities. He became seriously ill during his imprisonment. He was discharged only a few months ago. He leaves behind, I understand, a large family destitute of means of livelihood." Later, Mahatma Gandhi called Giri's family to Sabarmati Ashram. Giri's wife died in Bombay in 1946.

Another Freedom Struggle stalwart is Bhagatbir Tamang from Kurseong in Darjeeling district. He took an active part in the Non-Cooperation movement, organizing tea garden workers against the British and participating in decrying and denouncing colonial rule in India. He was arrested several times but detained for short periods. His last imprisonment, however, proved fatal. In August 1923, he was arrested and sent to the Darjeeling jail, where he died in January 1924.

Partiman Singh Lama, a close friend of Dalbahadur Giri, was a Forest Range Officer. At Gandhiji's call for the boycott of all things foreign, he quit government service and plunged into the Non-Cooperation movement. He organized activists in Kurseong and Mirik. Once, he rallied the people in Kurseong against Gandhiji's arrest. When the meeting got over, he was served with a notice asking him to refrain from leaving Kurseong town without the permission of the police.

Savitri Devi, the prominent Gorkha woman freedom fighter from Kurseong, played multiple roles in the, Swaraj struggle. She went from door to door in Kurseong and Siliguri urging the people to boycott foreign goods and led the burning of such goods in many places. She, along with her twelve Gorkha volunteers, was arrested at Siliguri and was put behind bars for three months in Darjeeling jail. After release, she was kept under strict vigilance. Such was the police vigil against her that for three years she was not able to move out of Kurseong town. The entry on her in the *Directory of Indian Women To-day* says:

> "Savitri Devi, first Nepali woman freedom fighter, b.1903. Her original name was Helen, Gandhiji renamed her 'Savitri Devi' when she went to Sabarmati ashram on his invitation. Her area of activity was Jhariya coal fields, Bankipur, Danapur, Patna, etc. Used to lead large processions protesting against the British regime. Lived in Ananda Bhavan also for some time. Helped Netaji Subhas Chandra Bose escape from imprisonment in Kurseong and migrate to Germany through Kabul."

Amid all this, the official gazette of the Darjeeling district duly underplayed the role played by the Gorkhas in the Non-Cooperation movement in the following words: "The Non-Co-operation Movement of 1921-22 was the first occasion in which hill men showed an interest in politics. It aroused excitement for a short time amongst tea garden labours and there was some boycott of foreign goods."

In the north-eastern region, Chhabilal Upadhyaya, Bhaktabahadur Pradhan, Dalbir Singh Lohar, and Pratap Singh Subba were the prominent freedom fighters among a host of Gandhian followers. Chhabilal Upadhyaya, reverently known as 'Assamko Gandhi', dedicated his life for the cause of social cultural, educational and political well-being of Assam through the Assam Association, which was the main political platform to promote Assam's development in various streams. When Gandhiji announced the Non-Cooperation Movement, Upadhyaya transformed the Assam Association into the Assam Provincial Congress Committee in 1921 and became one of its active members. He, along with his ardent supporters, hoisted the Congress flag at Behali Thana in 1942. The police arrested him and sent him to jail. During 1921-42 he underwent imprisonment and other sufferings many times. Chhabilal Upadhyaya was an ardent patriot and a distinguished freedom fighter.

Gorkhas in the INA: In the Anglo-Gorkha War of 1812-15, Gorkhas fought against the British. After the war, Balbhadra Kunwar spurned the offer to join the British, opting instead to strengthen the hand of Sikh Maharaja Ranjit Singh. Similarly, in World War II, many Gorkhas cut off their alliance with their British officers and joined the Indian National Army (INA) of Subhas Chandra Bose. Bose was the most formidable revolutionary leader of the Indian freedom movement. He was arrested by the British and was interned in Kurseong and Calcutta. He, however, managed to flee to Russia via Kabul and reached Germany. Hitler had been a diehard enemy of the British. One of his generals, Ribbentrop, welcomed Bose and assured all possible help in his struggle against the British in India.

At the Nymburg War Prisoners' Camp, Subhas Bose met a large number of Indian prisoners. Among them were 250 Gorkha soldiers. In Frankonberg Camp, there was another contingent of Indian prisoners. They all gladly agreed to join the Indian leader's Azad Hind Fauj. The Indian soldiers greeted him with the title of Netaji and saluted with a *Jai Hind*. The Gorkhas were among the first batch to join Netaji's unit, and the first martyr of Azad Hind Fauj was also a Gorkha soldier—Shyambahadur Thapa. At Khunisberg camp, while undergoing training, he contracted typhoid. It was Netaji's habit to attend to all the trainees personally, and so Shyambahadur breathed his last on Bose's lap. Thapa was cremated with martial honour. The same year Subhas Bose left Germany for Japan at the behest of Rashbehari Bose. He reached Singapore in 1942. On October 2, 1943, Subhas Bose formally announced the formation of the Arzi-Hukumat-e-Azad Hind (Government of Free India) and the Azad Hind Fauj (Indian National Army) and simultaneously declared war upon the Allied Forces. The first INA was set up under Captain Mohan Singh (1/14

Punjab Regiment). The first battalion, under the leadership of Shah Nawaz Khan, proceeded towards India via Kaladan valley in Arakan and Chin Hills of Burma. At one time the fauj accompanied by the Japanese soldiers marched towards Kohima, the present state capital of Nagaland. But the Japanese reverses in the international war theatre made the position of the INA very critical. Owing to many other setbacks, the INA was compelled to surrender to the British army. Shocked by the news, Netaji Subhas Chandra Bose left Burma for Saigon, from where he proceeded to Formosa on August 18, 1945. It is believed that Netaji was killed in an air crash en route.

After the surrender of the Azad Hind Fauj, the British Government tried Shah Nawaz Khan, Gurubux Singh Dhillon, Prem Sahgal and other generals on charges of treason. But the public and the Congress leaders denounced the trial. Ultimately, the British court changed its judgment and acquitted the INA stalwarts of the charges. But it is a matter of great concern that not a single text of Indian history has recorded the adverse judgment in the case against two Gorkha warriors, Major Durga Malla and Captain Dalbahadur Thapa, who were not excused on grounds of patriotism. Major Malla was executed at the Delhi Central Jail on August 25, 1944 and Captain Thapa on May 3, 1945.

Major Durga Malla was born on July 1, 1913 to Gangaram and Parvati Devi Malla at Doiwala village in Dehradun. Durga Malla joined the 2/1 battalion of the Gorkha Rifles in 1931. He was promoted to the rank of Signal Havildar and sent to the war zone in 1941. By September of that year, all the Gorkha battalions had reached Malaya. In December, a group of Indian soldiers lost themselves in the jungle of Malaya, two of them being Captain Mohan Singh and Havildar Durga Malla. No sooner had they come out of the jungle than they were captured by the Japanese and imprisoned at Singapore. Later, they were handed over to Subhas Bose.

In the INA, Durga Malla was given the rank of major and was entrusted with the task of Intelligence. He was posted on the Burma border. He had to send information regarding matters of strategic importance to the INA headquarters in Rangoon. While collecting information about the enemy camp at Ukhrul in Manipur, he was captured by the British army and deported to Delhi. After a trial of five months at the Red Fort, he was sent to the gallows.

Captam Dalbahadur Thapa was the son of Santabir Thapa of Barakotha village of Kangra district. He was born in 1907. He joined 2/1 GR and achieved the rank of jamadar in the Indian Army in 1939. During World War II he was sent to the Far East. While fighting with the Japanese, he was captured and imprisoned in Singapore. After the formation of the INA, he was handed over to Subhas Bose, under whom he vowed to free India. He was made a captain and the commander of the Bahadur Group of the guerrilla force. While fighting in the Kohima-Manipur front, he was captured by the British on June 28, 1944. During his trial at the Red Fort in Delhi, he was coaxed in recanting and flogged for thirteen months, but he proved a true son of mother India and smiling, he ascended the scaffold on May 3, 1945.

There are hundreds of Gorkhas who played important roles in the INA, but the names of two Thakurs needs mention here They are INA Commander Purna Singh Thakur and INA maestro Ram Singh Thakur.

Purna Singh Thakur was among the first volunteers of the INA. Born in 1909 at Dharamshala, the son of Balbir Singh Thakur, he was recruited in 2/1 GR in 1928 and was a major in the Indian Army In World War II, he was detailed to Malaya. While fighting with the Japanese, he was trapped at Jitra town of Malaya and captured. He surrendered his platoon to the Japanese. They directed him to collect the names of all the Indian war prisoners from the different camps. He went to

Penang and Olaster for this work under Captain Mohan Singh, who was also one of his co-prisoners. They enlisted the names from various Gorkha regiments, including 2/1, 2/2 and 2/9 GRs. An army was formed with these prisoners and the Japanese commander directed them to attack the British on the island of Obin. The British were overcome and surrendered their 70,000 soldiers to Japanese General Fujiwara Later, Subhas Rose formed the INA with many of these POWs in the ranks. Purna Singh was given the charge of recruiting and training the volunteers. In June 1942, he represented/the, Gorkha troops at the historical Bangkok Conference. In May 1945 he, along with his men, were taken prisoners in Rangoon and brought to Calcutta and then to Delhi. He was tried and sentenced to rigorous imprisonment of seven years at the Red Fort.

To quote from General Mohan Singh's *Leaves from My Diary:* "18 March 1946—Purna has also been taken away. He has been awarded seven years' RI. This Gorkha Officer was one of my very fast companions who fought very bravely by my side. He and his colleagues have proved to the world that the barriers that have been built by the British to rob India of her very brave fighting men are but artificial. They can be removed at any time and Gorkhas, in spite of British efforts, will remain the pride of the Indian ...... The part played by the Gorkhas in the INA. is something to be proud of."

On August 15, 1947, Purna Singh, Fateh Khan and Singhara Singh were released from Lahore Central Jail.

The other Thakur, Ram Singh, was born in Dharamshala in a military family in August 1914. His father was Dalip Singh Thakur Ram Singh learned classical music at home from his grandfather Nathuchand Thakur. After passing Middle School, he joined 2/1 Gorkha Rifles in January 1927 as a boy-recruit in the Band Unit. In the platoon, he was trained to play in the brass band, the string band and the dance band by Hudson and Danis. In 1941 he was made Company Havildar Major and was sent to the Singapore unit. The same year, in December, the Japanese attacked Malaya and the British force had to retreat. But some soldiers imprisoned by the Japanese were handed over to Subhas Bose for his Azad Hind Fauj. After the setting up of Azad Hind Radio, Ram Singh Thakur was assigned to act as music director in the Singapore and Rangoon stations. He composed, numerous patriotic songs, among them, *Kadam kadam badaye ja; Azad hind ke jawan, Lahara yeh tiranga pyara, Ham dilli, dilli jayenge,* and *Shubha sukha chain ki barsa barse.* Subhas Bose was a fan of Ram Singh's songs. On January 23, 1944, the Band Unit of the Azad Hind Fauj celebrated Netaji's birthday and on the occasion, Subhas Bose himself honoured Ram Singh Thakur with a gold medal and a violin.

In May 1945, Rangoon was again captured by the Allied Force Ram Singh, along with his troops, was taken into custody and brought to India. He was tried and would have been hanged for the treason but the British lost the case against Sahgal-Shahnawaz-Dhillon and he was released alone with the trio.

In 1946 Ram Singh made a courtesy call on Jawaharlal Nehru. India's would-be prime minister asked him to organize an INA orchestra troupe and disseminate patriot songs throughout the country. He did so for a year. Ram Singh composed the tune for Iqbal's words, *Sare jahan se achchha Hindustan hamara,* as part of this errand.

On the historic day of August 15, 1947, Ram Singh Thakur was summoned once more by Nehru to sing a patriotic song. Early morning on the day India shook off her colonial rule, Thakur and his orchestra sang from the ramparts of Lal Qila:

> *Shubha sukha chain ki barsa barse, Bharat bhagya hai jaga*
> *Punjab Sind Gujrata Maratha Dravida Utkala Banga*
> *Chanchal Sagar Vindhya Himalaya Nila Yamuna Ganga*

Tere nita guna gayen, tujh se jivan payen
Sab tan pay en aasha
Suraj banker jagpar chamke Bharata naam subhaga
Jaya ho jaya ho jaya ho jaya ho
Bharata naam subhaga

Ram Singh played the tune on the violin which had been presented to him by none but Subhas Bose himself. The lyric was most probably written by Mumtaz Hussain. Later, the song was changed to incorporate Rabindranath Tagore's lyrics, but Ram Singh's tune was retained. It is a matter of coincidence that today we have our national anthem written and composed by two Thakurs: one Rabindranath Thakur and the other, Ram Singh Thakur.

After independence, Ram Singh was given a post in the Provincial Armed Constabulary band by the Uttar Pradesh Government. After serving for 26 years, he retired in 1974 as a Deputy Superintendent of Police. In 1995, the Sikkim Government honoured him with the prestigious 'Mitrasen Thapa Puraskar' at Gangtok. Earlier in 1977, the UP Government had given him a public ovation in Lucknow, where M.C. Reddy, the then Governor of Uttar Pradesh sent a message: "Captain Ram Singh's personality is a novel blending of art, patriotism and national spirit. He was a gallant soldier of the INA and a close associate of Netaji Subhas Chandra Bose. He is at his best when singing national songs, and at whatever function he appears, he emerges as the centre of people's attention and affection. His unassuming and modest character is the whole mystery of his single success."

In the long list of freedom fighter and martyrs, at least three more people deserve to be mentioned here, and they are of Savitri Thapa and Indreni Thapa of the Northeast and an unknown boy of Singapore. All three of them were juvenile fighters, and so, of course, their official reports are not on record.

Mrs Mayadevi Chettri, former Rajya Sabha member from Darjeeling, has authored a book titled *Swatantrata*

Sangram, which mentions the sacrifices of these two girls. It is said that one day Netaji Subhas Chandra Bose noticed a British tank coming forward and was in a fix because there was none around to check its advance. Then, Savitri and Indreni came forward to offer their services. They assured Netaji that they would stop the tank. Carrying camouflaged bombs on their bodies, they lay down in a trench and covered themselves with grass. When the tank ran over them, the bombs detonated and destroyed the tank.

As for the unnamed boy, he was the son of a milkmaid in Singapore and died while pelting stones at British soldiers. His story was published in *Dinman*, a popular Hindi weekly of India.

Hence, whether it is Gorkha soldiers or singer, laypeople or children, all have shown their mettle at a time when their country needed them the most.

The Naval Mutiny: The Royal Indian Naval Mutiny of 1946 is not discussed much in the history of our freedom movement. On the February 18, 1946, the ratings of the Royal Indian Navy arose in open mutiny. Many opine that if the Sepoy Mutiny of 1857 is considered the first war in the fight for freedom, the 1946 naval rebellion was the last. N.S. Bose writes in his *The Indian National Movement: An Outline:* "The revolt of the ratings was of great significance. This was the first time since 1857 that a section of the defence forces had openly rebelled against the British on an issue that was essentially political"

The mutiny was so comprehensive that it involved more than 78 warships and 20,000 sailors from Bombay to Karachi. Initially, the mutineers of warship HMIS *Talwar* in Bombay and HMIS *Hindusthan* in Karachi revolted in unison. Two Indian Gorkhas played a leading role in this uprising. Chandra Kumar Sharma of Maligaon, Assam, and Pushpa Kumar Ghisingh of Kurseong, Darjeeling, aroused the *esprit de corps* among co-workers. Chandra Kumar was the leading stocker onboard

Hindusthan, while Pushpa Kumar was an electrician on the *Talwar.*

What riled the shipmen was the fact that the British officers treated Indian ratings as slaves, freely discriminating between natives and foreigners, Hindus and Muslims. Caste, creed and racial discriminations repulsed the Indians, who were on the brink of winning independence. For instance, an Indian Gorkha officer on HMIS *Jamuna,* Lieutenant Mani Ghisingh, was denied entry to the officers' mess because he was a native. The mutineers boycotted food first, to which a British Commanding officer, a certain Mr King, bitingly remarked: "Beggars can't be choosers." The Indian ratings would have killed him there had he not fled. Admiral Rattray, Flag Officer, Bombay, intervened to say that King would be replaced by another officer, but the ratings objected and shouted, "No British, no British any more".

On February 19, the ratings assembled on the *Talwar.* Action plans were made. None of the rating would join the duties. First they replaced the Union Jack with the tricolour. Pushpa Kumar himself removed the British flag. Then he led a procession from Breakwater to Signal School. The following day, another procession was organized. It was led by M.S. Khan, chief signalman and President of the Naval Central Strike Committee. The British tried to suppress the mutiny and there was some exchange of fire.

On the midnight of February 22, at the behest of top Congress leaders, the agitators withdrew their strike. They surrendered before the Congress, but not before the British. The British sent the mutineers to jail. M.S. Khan, Pushpa Kumar, Chandra Kumar, A.K. Rai, R. Charles, Akbar Ali and a host of strikers and processionists were imprisoned at the Miller War Prisoners' Camp in Karachi for four months.

On May 31, 1946, the *Karachi Observer* published a news items detailing how Chandra Kumar Sharma had argued that ratings were made to do things forbidden by religion and treated no better than slaves. The news items said: "The Indian ratings live and move in an atmosphere of slavery. Educated, intelligent and capable, they are yet made to suffer constantly both physical anguish and mental torture by reason of their colour and nationality. .. .(This was) the cumulative effect of the numerous instances of racial discrimination from which they have suffered doing the manual jobs of cleaning lavatories and mess tables for the Royal Navy Ratings which they have been repeatedly forced to perform. Leading Stocker Chandra Kumar stated before the RIN Inquiry Commission yesterday."

National leaders like Mahatma Gandhi, Nehru and Sardar Patel put pressure on the British Government to release the mutineers without a court martial. Chandra Kumar Sharma was released without standing trial but his service was terminated. He returned home to Maligaon, Assam and served as manager in the NF Railway Marine Shop at Guwahati. After his retirement, he was shot dead by extremists on February 6, 1989.

Pushpa Kumar Ghisingh cleverly managed the Court Martial Order. He was acquitted and served for a few months more on the Jamuna before retiring on September 8, 1946.

M.S. Khan, the president of the Striking Committee, was, however, taken by the British to some unknown maritime destination, where he mysteriously disappeared.

India Wins Her Freedom

August 15, 1947, is a red-letter day in the history of India. After nearly a century-long struggle, India won freedom from her colonial masters. But there was mixed feelings that day. It brought freedom but also partition—division both of territory and the armed forces. India was divided on the ground of religion, while the Gorkhas were divided due to their valour. Independence thus was ironical for the Gorkhas. For long they had lived together and fought together. Now they would be differentiated into the British Gurkhas and the Indian Gorkhas. The brave soldiers were like a commodity, the subject of a barter between two powers.

The service of Gorkhas during war and peace was highly appreciated by everyone. The King-emperor of the British Empire and the Prime Minister of Free India were equally determined to have the Gorkha soldiers on their side.

However, in his *Discovery of India,* Nehru betrayed his real opinion about the Gorkhas when he wrote: "The Gorkhas of Nepal were splendid and disciplined soldiers, the equals, if not the superiors, of any troops that the East India Company could produce. Although completely in feudal organization, their attachment to their homeland was great, and this sentiment made them formidable fighters in its defence. They gave a fright to the British, but made no difference to the issue of the main struggle in India."

The crucial historical point here is that the British recruited Gorkhas not only from Nepal, but also from Bhagsu, Simla, Dehradun, Kumaon, Garhwal and Darjeeling, places that had become Indian territory after the Sugauli Treaty. Gorkhas from these places played a significant role in the 'main struggle' of India, since they considered India as their motherland. But from his book, it seems Nehru thought Gorkhas came only from Nepal.

Nevertheless, as Kanchanmoy Mazumdar points out, "Jawaharlal had agreed to issue on behalf of the Congress an authoritative declaration that the Gorkhas in India were an integral section of the Indian population and that they and the Indians were like brothers."

Nehru accepted the view that independent India needed a strong and powerful army. He wanted that the Gorkha battalions should be retained in the post-war Indian Army and they should be officered by the Indian Officer."

Still Nehru wavered about unequivocally describing the Gorkhas as Indians. His declaration that "Gorkhas in India are an integral section of Indian population" yet "they should be officered by Indian officers" is a self-controversial statement.

Even up to the March 1947, Nehru reiterated India's refusal to give the Gorkhas to the British Government on the ground that they would be deployed for an imperialistic agenda. However, Nehru's concern for the Gorkhas was governed by India's own situation at home. The government had to weigh any proposal for a change in the system of government in India in the backdrop of the army having almost 60 per cent Muslims in its ranks. Nehru had already told Viceroy Wavell that India would need a first-class army when she won her freedom.

In the Constituent Assembly, Dambar Singh Gurung, the first MP from Darjeeling, had assured Nehru, "Today the Gorkhas led by the All India Gorkha League are pledged to fight alongside the Congress for the complete independence of India; they also stand for the Indian Union. India is at the threshold of freedom, but not yet free; and should ever the struggle for freedom have to be renewed, the Gorkhas will be at the vanguard of the fight. In the free India of the future, the Gorkhas will do their share of the honourable task of the country's defence."

This assurance of the Gorkhas came when the Congress party was not in a position to take the Sikhs into confidence and was in a dilemma regarding the inclusion of East Punjab in the Indian Union because of the Sikhs' persistent demand for an autonomous state. Thus, Nehru was not inclined to give up the Gorkhas to the British.

After independence, the division of the Indian Army between the British and India was inevitable and several regiments, like the Sikh, Jat, Maratha regiments, the Assam Rifles and Jammu & Kashmir Rifles, proved no problem. But the Gorkha Regiment was a bone of contention between the two powers.

In a dramatic manoeuvre, the British Government succeeded in getting four regiments of the Gorkhas for the British Army by awarding India the Andaman & Nicobar Islands, to which Burma and Pakistan were also claimants. Thus the decision to have the 2nd, 6th, 7th and 10th Gorkha Rifles in the British Army and the remaining six in the Indian Army was made on August 8, 1947.

The status of the Gorkhas in the Indian Army was open to myths till late. When the Indian contingents of UN peace-keeping troops reached Congo in 1962, breakaway leader Moise Tshombe erroneously described the Gorkha soldiers of the Indian contingent as 'hired soldiers'. But the Government of India, through V.K. Krishna Menon, the then minister of defence, categorically stated that all the Gorkha soldiers serving in the Indian Army were first rate citizens of India.

Gorkhas in Defence

After the achievement of independence, the Gorkhas of India are engaged in various units of nation-building. Defence is their prime and principal province. At the time of partition, while rescuing the trapped and stranded Indians on the border, Major Ramsaran Karki, Captain Premsingh Bista, Lieutenant Raghubir Thapa, Subedar-Major Bhimsingh Mahat, Naik Bhagwan Singh Karki, Sub-Officers Man Bahadur Thapa, Bhimsingh Rana, Mohansingh Thapa, Rifleman Gopalsingh Sahi and many other Gorkhas became martyrs.

Soon after the partition, Kashmir became the hotspot of conflict for the two new nations. In the middle of October 1947, Muslim raiders from the Murree and Hazara Hills strode eastward into Kashmir. They stormed up the Jhelum river valley and taking Muzaffarabad and Domel went on to sack Baramulla. They left a trail of murder and rapine and some 3,000 dead. Eleven days after the sack of Baramulla, the Gorkha troops regained the town and advanced up the Jhelum valley as far as Uri.

The Pakistani Army joined the fray. A Gorkha battalion, sent south from Uri to Urusanallah climbed nearly 11,000 ft up the Pir Kanti ridge and finished up with a khukuri charge that accounted for 54 enemy dead on the ground. Their own casualties were 7 dead and 51 wounded.

During the winter of 1947-48, the Pakistani raiders advanced up to the Indus valley through Gilgit. They took Kargil and Dras. In May and June, Gorkhas reached there by air. The following month, another company of Gorkhas flew in. The 5th Gorkhas took part in the operation to reopen the route through Kargil. A serious battle was fought which left 48 Gorkhas dead, 86 wounded and 37 missing. The 5th Gorkha received five gallantry awards in this action.

The Gorkhas have received Vir Chakras playing their parts in two 'Police actions.' The first concerned the 5th Gorkhas, and was the Indian Army's entry into the South Indian state of Hyderabad in order to force the Nizam to accede to India and the second was the action in Nagaland where the tribes were up in armed revolt. The 11th GR was revived at this point.

In 1961, the 1/8th Gorkhas were up in India's remotest outposts of Ladakh on the far side of Leh. They were still there when the Chinese attacked them in 1962 by the Lake Pangong. In July and August, the Gorkhas fought back against the Chinese. In this war, Major Dhansingh Thapa received the Param Vir Chakra, the highest gallantry award of India. However, it was only the prelude to a massive attack in October 1962.

In the Indo-Pak wars and Indo-China wars, thousands

of Gorkhas gave their lives for the country. Even today, Gorkha corpses regular come home from various parts of India, heroes who have died battling extremists and terrorists. Despite all these, the Gorkhas' contribution to the national cause is often glossed over, which is rather unfortunate.

Rabindranath Thakur has rightly described India as a great ocean of humanity where people of diverse origins, creeds and language groups are mingled to contribute to a composite Indian culture. No one can with certainty pinpoint when a particular tribe came to India and first settled here. As far as the Gorkha/Nepali or the Khas-Kirat tribe is concerned, many scriptures and chronicles talk of the existence of this race in time immemorial.

At present a large segment of Nepali-speaking people are settled in every part of India from Kashmir to Assam. They have been living in India from before and since the signing of the Treaty of Sugauli in 1815. There are also records to show that the Gorkhas had made permanent settlements in Assam long before it was conquered by the British. Clearing the forest and bringing the land under their plough, they became first-rate agriculturists and many of them permanent settled down in the region when the British established their military cantonments, a direct result of Gorkhas being encouraged to join the British Indian Army from 1814.

The annexation of Darjeeling and Dooars by the British and the subsequent growth of the tea industry attracted a large number of people, especially from Eastern Nepal, as these parts were closely connected. In the Dooars tea plantations, Nepalis from the adjacent areas and Adivasis from Bihar, Chhotanagpur, Chhattisgarh and Orissa arrived in droves. After the merger of Sikkim with India in 1975, the Gorkhas and tribes of different ethnic origins having common characteristics have abounded in this region.

A good number of Gorkhas live in the Doon valley and the adjoining areas of Uttar Pradesh. They have been here since the region was ceded to the British by Nepal after the Anglo-Nepal War of 1812-14. Following the example of the British, many Indian rajas, like those of Kashmir and Punjab, recruited the Gorkhas in their armies and police forces. Since then, many Gorkhas have become permanent settlers in areas of Kashmir and Punjab too. The Gorkhas in India have been playing a constructive role in the process of nation-building for century together.

If the Gorkhas participated in the work of nation-building prior to 1947, they have equally been active in the task since the achievement of independence. Their role as soldiers in the Indian Army of free India has remained equally distinguished. In various Indo-Pak wars and the border conflicts of 1947, 1965, and 1971 and against China in 1962, the Gorkhas have died defending the country. And whenever the country has needed to prove its military prowess, it has turned to the Gorkhas. On various occasions, Gorkhas have been deployed in the UN peace-keeping assignments.

But the Gorkhas who consolidated India, unified it as one nation, have no home of their own. For them, there cannot be a bigger irony than helping to build a huge mansion, only to find they have to room to live in.

Another paradox is that more than a quarter million Gorkha Adivasis work in the tea plantations that cover 1.03 lakh hectares of land in North Bengal, but neither a single tea bush belongs to them, nor an inch of land. They are only the hired labourers of the private companies, in many ways as beholden to their employers as they were once to the East India Company.

The Gorkhas are facing a number of crises today. Their identity problem is the main one. A separate state of their own would identify them as a distinct Indian community. Dr Ranju Dhamala, a political scientist, writes, "The principle of integration while maintaining the distinctiveness of each group has been the hallmark of the nation-building process. The Indian polity, instead of advancing the melting-pot theory, has adopted the salad-bowl principle. Such an attitude has enabled each group to maintain their distinctiveness and at the same time add to the growth of the country. The importance of community-based identities in Indian context is explicable in view of the richness of the differential markers of the communities and also their transmission to the plural field of the Indian nation as a whole. Living in India the Nepali-speaking community has conspicuously retained its positioned life perspective, cultural world-view and at the same time contributed significantly to the plural perception of the country as whole. This is an ongoing process".

This ongoing process is more meaningful in the actualization of the long standing demand of the Indian Gorkhas for a state under the provision of Article 3 (A) of the Indian Constitution. It would be an achievement of not only a particular region, but would work as a boost to the entire people of the country for legitimizing their distinctiveness in the national discourse for the enrichment of the country as a whole and ushering in a new meaning of what India is and can be.

The Indian Gorkhas have been demanding a separate state in India for over a century now. But having no political strength at the Centre, their demand has no ear. The year 2007 marked one hundred years of the Gorkhas aspiring for an administrative unit that would put governance in their hands. The first memorandum on the issue was submitted by the Hillmen's Association in 1907, the second memorandum submitted by the same Hillmen's Association of Darjeeling in 1917. That paper argued:

> "We live in an absolutely different world from the rest of the people of Bengal. Geographically no greater contrast is possible than that between the mountainous Darjeeling District and the plains

> of Bengal. Racially there is an equal dissimilarity for the great mass of our population is Mongolian and akin to the people beyond the Himalayas rather than to those of India. Historically we have until recent years lived a life entirely apart. The Darjeeling District, except the Kalimpong Sub-Division, was gifted by or annexed from the Kingdom of Sikkim last century; the Kalimpong Sub-Division and the Dooars were Bhutanese till about fifty years ago Our humble petition therefore, is that in laying down plans for the future, the Government should aim at the creation of separate unit comprising the present Darjeeling District with the portion of Jalpaiguri District which was annexed from Bhutan in 1865.... "

The memorandum of 1917 was signed by:

1. S.W. Laden La	2. Khadga Bahadur Chhetri
3. Yensing Sitling	4. Prem Singh Kumai
5. Meghbir Singh	6. Lachman Singh
7. Nar Prasad Kumai	8. Deonidhi Upadhyaya & others.

Different social institutions and political parties have submitted memoranda time and again, postulating the same demand. Some of these are the Hillmen's Association (1930, 1934), Darjeeling District Committee CPI (1947), Uttarakhanda Pradesh (1948), All India Gorkha League (1952), Darjeeling Zila Shramik Sangh (1955), Darjeeling District Congress Committee (1968, 1986), Pranta Parishad (1981) and the Gorkha National Liberation Front (1983).

Now, the Bharatiya Gorkha Parisangh, a national federation of Gorkha organizations and Gorkha people, has come forward in search of a suitable homeland within the country. It proposes Darjeeling district and Dooars as the most suitable and viable location for the creation of a separate state for the Gorkhas of India. The Parisangh is also of the firm opinion that nothing short of a full-fledged statehood for Darjeeling-Dooars region will meet the aspirations of the Gorkhas of India.

BIBLIOGRAPHY

Acharya, Ghanashyam, *The Gorkhas of Manipur,* Manipur Gorkha Welfare Union, 1999.

Agrawal, Hem Narayan. *Nepal: A Country Study in Constitutional Change.* New Delhi: Oxford & IBH, 1980.

Austin, Ian and Thakur Nahar Singh Jasol. (eds.) *The Mewar Encyclopedia.*

Austin, Ian. (1999). *Mewar—The World's Longest Serving Dynasty.* Roli Books, Delhi/The House of Mewar.

Baral, Lok Raj. *"Nepal in 1986: Problems of Political Management,"* Asian Survey, 27, No. 2, February 1987, 173-80.

Baral, Lok Raj. *"Nepal in 1987: Politics Without Power,"* Asian Survey, 28, No. 2, February 1988, 172-79.

Barthorp, Michael. (2002) *Afghan Wars and the North-West Frontier 1839-1947.* Cassell.

Bhandari, Purushottam, *Freedom Movement and Role of Indian Nepalese 1800-1950,* Mrs Rama Bhandari, Jagi Road, Nowgaon, Assam, 1996.

British Broadcasting Commission Staff (2 June 2007). *"Gurkha tells of citizenship joy"*. BBC News, 2 June 2007.

Chappell, Mike (1993). *The Gurkhas.* Oxford: Osprey Publishing.

Chauhan, Dr. Sumerendra Vir Singh. (1996). *The Way of Sacrifice: The Rajputs, Pages 28-30, Graduate Thesis, South Asian Studies Department,* Dr. Joseph T. O'Connell, Professor Emeritus, University of Toronto, Toronto, Ontario Canada.

Chhetri, Padam, *Turaka Nepaliharu, Pradip Chhetri, Brahman Para,* Tura, Meghalaya 1993.

Cross, J.P & Buddhiman Gurung. (2002) *Gurkhas at War: Eyewitness Accounts from World War II to Iraq.* Greenhill Books.

Davenport, Hugh. (1975). *The Trials and Triumphs of the Mewar Kingdom.* Maharana Mewar Charitable Foundation, Udaipur.

Dhanalaxmi, Ravuri. *British Attitude to Nepal's Relations with Tibet and China, 1814-1914.* Chandigarh, India: Bahri, 1981.

Dhikari, Krishna Kant. *Nepal under Jang Bahadur,* 1846-1877. Kathmandu: Buku, 1984.

Ember, Carol & Ember, Melvin. (2003). *Encyclopedia of Sex and Gender: Men and Women in the World's Cultures.* Springer.

Farwell, Byron, *The Gurkhas,* Penguin Books Ltd., Middlesex, England, 1984

Farwell, Byron. (1985). *The Gurkhas.* W.W. Norton & Co.

Forbes Duncan, *Johny Gurkha,* Vikas Publishing House, Delhi 6, 1974.

Gaige, Frederick H. *Regionalism and National Unity in Nepal.* Berkeley: University of California Press, 1975.

Ghising, Kumar, *Doonghati-Nalapam,* Pines Prakashan, Sonada, Darjeeling, 1982.

Gorkhas Imagined: LB. *Rai in Translation,* Mukti Prakashan, 2009.

Goswami, C.G. and M.N. Mathur. *Mewar and Udaipur.* Himnashu Publications, Udaipur-New Delhi.

Goswami, Prodyot Kumar. *Indian Currency and Exchange,* 1835-1940. New Delhi: Milind, 1983.

Gould, Tony. (2000). *Imperial Warriors - Britain and the Gurkhas.* Granta Books.

Griffiths, Neil. Gurkha Walking books: *'Hebridean Gurkha; 'Gurkha Highlander'; 'Gurkha Reiver'.* Neil takes a Scottish cross-country walk with Gurkhas every year to raise funds for the Gurkha Welfare Trust.

Gurney, Gene. Kingdoms of Asia, the Middle East, and Africa: An Illustrated Encyclopedia of Ruling Monarchs from Ancient Times to the Present. New York: Crown, 1986.

Gurung, Chandra Bahadur, *British Medals & Gurkhas,* Himalayan Yeti Nepalese Assn., U.K., 1998.

Gurung, Narbahadur, *Darjeeling, Kamal Kutir,* Kalmipong, Darjeeling, 1971.

Heck, Douglas. *"Nepal in 1980: The Year of the Referendum,"* Asian Survey, 21, No. 2, February 1981, 181-87.

Jain, M.S. *Emergence of a New Aristocracy in Nepal, 1837-58.* Agra, India: Sri Ram Mehar, 1972.

Joshi, Bhuwan Lal, and Leo E. Rose. *Democratic Innovations in Nepal: A Case Study of Political Acculturation.* Berkeley: University of California Press, 1966.

Kapuria, R.S. *The Indian Rupee: A Study in Retrospect and Prospect.* Bombay: Vora, 1967.

Khadka, Narayan. *"The Political Economy of the Food Crisis in Nepal,"* Asian Survey, 25, No. 9, September 1985, 943-62.

Khanal, Y.N. *"Nepal in 1984: A Year of Complacence,"* Asian Survey, 25, No. 2, February 1985, 180-86.

Kharga, Khiroda, *Amor Adarsha Jiwani, Book I, II, III, Rukmini Chhetri,* Kurseong, Darjeeling, 1988-91.

Koirala, Niranjan. *"Nepal in 1989: A Very Difficult Year,"* Asian Survey, 30, No. 2, February 1990, 136-43.

Kulke, Hermann, and Dietmar Rothermund. *A History of India.* Totowa, New Jersey: Barnes and Noble, 1986.

Kumar, Satish. *Rana Polity in Nepal:* Origin and Growth. New York: Asia, 1967.

Lama, R.P., Jagat Chhetri (Eds.), *Dal Bahadur Gin Smriti Grantha,* Nepali Sahitya Sammelan, Darjeeling, 1988.

Latimer, Jon. (2004). Burma: *The Forgotten War,* London: John Murray.

Lévi, Sylvain. *Le Nepal: Etude historique d'un royaume hindou.* (3 vols.) Paris: E Leroux, 1905-8.

Magan Pathik, *Azad Hind Fauj Ke Ye Gorkha Bir,* Imperial Printing Press, Dharamashala, HI3, 1991.

Misra, Shashi P. *P.P. Koirala: A Case Study in Third World Democratic Leadership.* Bhubaneswar, India: Konark, 1985.

Mitra, Debala. *Buddhist Monuments.* Calcutta: Sahitya Samsad, 1971.

Mojumdar, Kanchanmoy. *Anglo-Nepalese Relations in the Nineteenth Century.* Calcutta: K.L. Mukhopadhyay, 1973.

Moktan, R., *Sikkim-Darjeeling: A Compendium of Documents,* Sumaralaya, Kalimpong, Darjeeling, 2004.

Naravane, M. S. (2006). *Battles of the honourable East India Company: Making of the Raj.* APH Publishing, pp. 189-191.

Nehru, Jawaharlal, *Discovery of India,* Oxford University Press, 1993.

O'Malley, L.S.S., *Darjeeling District Gazetteer 1907,* Gyan Publishing House, New Delhi.

Panday, Devendra Raj. "*Nepal in 1981: Stagnation Amidst Change,* Asian Survey, 22, No. 2, February 1982, 155-62.

Parker, John. (2005). *The Gurkhas: The Inside Story of the World's Most Feared Soldiers*. Headline Book Publishing.

Parmanand. *The Nepali Congress since its Inception: A Critical Assessment*. Delhi: B.R. Publishing, 1982.

Pemble, John. (2009). *Forgetting and remembering Britain's Gurkha War. Asian Affairs, 40(3), 361-376.* Abstract available here (retrieved 12-22-2009).

Pemble, John. (2009). *Forgetting and remembering Britain's Gurkha War. Asian Affairs, 40(3), 361-376.* Abstract available here (retrieved 12-22-2009). Contains a historiographical analysis of the Gurkha "legend."

Pemble, John. *The Invasion of Nepal: John Company at War.* Oxford: Oxford University Press, 1971.

Petech, Luciano. *Mediaeval History of Nepal* (ca. 750-1480). (2d ed.) (Serie orientate, toma 54.) Rome: Institutio Italiano per il Medio ed Estremo Oriente, 1984.

Poddar, Prem and Anmole Prasad. (2009). *Gorkhas Imagined: IB. Rai in Transaltion*. Mukti Prakasham.

Purushottam Sham Shere J B Rana. (1998). *Jung Bahadur Rana-The Story of His Rise and Glory.*

Rai, MP., *Bir Jatiko Amar Kahani,* Ajako Sikkim Prakashan, Gantok, Sikkim, 1992.

Regmi, Dilli Raman. *Ancient Nepal.* (3d ed.) Calcutta: K.L. Mukhopadhyay, 1969.

Regmi, Dilli Raman. *Medieval Nepal.* (4 vols.) Calcutta: K.L. Mukhopadhyay, 1965-66.

Risley, H.H., *A Gazetteer of Sikkim,* Sikkim Nature Conservation Foundation, Gantok, 1894.

Rose, Leo E. Nepal: *Strategy for Survival.* Berkeley: University of California Press, 1971.

Rose, Leo E., and Bhuwan Lai Joshi. *Democratic Innovations in Nepal.* Berkeley: University of California Press, 1966.

Rose Leo E., and John T. Scholz. *Nepal: Profile of a Himalayan Kingdom.* Boulder, Colorado: Westvlew Press, 1930.

Rose, Leo E., and Margaret W. Fisher. *The Politics of Nepal: Persistence and Change in an Asian Monarchy.* Ithaca: Cornell University Press, 1970.

Seear, Mike. (2002). *With The Gurkhas in the Falklands.*

Shah, Sukhdev. *"Developing an Economy: Nepal's Experience,"* Asian Survey, 21, No. 10, October 1981, 1060-79.

Sinha, Gokul, *A Treatise on Nepali Language,* Uttaranchal Prakashan, Darjeeling, 1978.

Sir Mark Tully's presentation of the Indian Army during the Second World War Bharat-Rakshak.

Slusser, Mary Shephers. *Nepal Mandaia: A Cultural Study of the Kathmandu Valley.* (2 vols.) Princeton: Princeton University Press, 1982.

Spear, Percival. *A History of India.* New York: Penguin Books, 1981.

Stiller, Ludwig. *The Rise of the House of Gorkha: A Study in the Unification of Nepal.* New Delhi: Manjusri, 1973.

Stiller, Ludwig. *The silent Cry: The People of Nepal, 1816-1839.* Kathmandu: Sahayogi Prakashan 1976.

Sunar, Er. Pradip, *Kan war Jeevan, Subba I.K., The Gorkhas of Mizoram,* Vol. 1, Mizoram Gorkha Students' Union, Aizawal, 1999.

Thapar, Romila. *A History of India.* New York: Penguin, 1966.

Tod, James & Crooke, William, (eds.) (1920). *Annals and Antiquities of Rajasthan.* 3 Volumes. Motilal Banarsidass Publishers Pvt. Ltd., Delhi. Reprinted 1994.

Tucci, Giuseppe. *Nepal: The Discovery of the Malla.* (Trans., Lovett Edwards.) New York: Dutton, 1962.

Tucci, Sandro. (1985). *Gurkhas.* Published by H.Hamilton.

Tyagi, Sushila. *Indo-Nepalese Relations, 1858-1914.* Delhi: D.K. Publishing, 1974.

Upadhyaya, Bishnulal, Chhabilal Upadhyaya, *Kulbahadur Chhetri,* Margherita, Assam, 1985.

Upadhyaya, Bishnulal, *Hamra Swatnatrata Senani,* Nepali Sahitya Praehar Samiti, Siliguri, 1991.

Upadhyaya, Bishnulal, NEFA, Publication Divisior, *Ministry of Information and Broadcasting, Government of India, 1965.*

Upadhyaya, Bishnulal, *Nepal and the Gurkhas, Her Majesty's Stationery Office,* London, 1965.

Upadhyaya, Bishnulal, *Shaheed Durga Malla,* Lok Sabha Secretariat, New Delhi 2004.

Wright, Daniel (ed.). *Vamsavali: history of Nepal. (Trans., Munshi Shew Shunker Singh and Pundi Gunanand.)* Kathmandu: Nepal Antiquated Book Publishers, 1972.